Also by Nico Tortorella

*all of it is you.*

# SPACE BETWEEN

# SPACE BETWEEN

## EXPLORATIONS OF LOVE, SEX, AND FLUIDITY

# NICO TORTORELLA

CROWN
NEW YORK

All rights reserved.
Published in the United States by Crown, an imprint of Random House, a
division of Penguin Random House LLC, New York.
crownpublishing.com

CROWN and the Crown colophon are registered trademarks of Penguin
Random House LLC.

This is a work of nonfiction. Nonetheless, some of the names and
identifying details of the individuals discussed have been changed. Any
resulting resemblance to persons living or dead is entirely coincidental
and unintentional.

Library of Congress Cataloging-in-Publication Data
Names: Tortorella, Nico, author.
Title: Space between / Nico Tortorella.
Description: First edition. | New York : Crown, 2019
Identifiers: LCCN 2019005466 | ISBN 9780525576730 (hardcover)
Subjects: LCSH: Tortorella, Nico. | Sexual minorities—Identity. | Gender
    identity. | Sexual orientation. | Non-monogamous relationships.
Classification: LCC HQ73 .T67 2019 | DDC 305.3—dc23
LC record available at https://lccn.loc.gov/2019005466

ISBN 978-0-525-57673-0
Ebook ISBN 978-0-525-57675-4

PRINTED IN THE UNITED STATES OF AMERICA

10 9 8 7 6 5 4 3 2 1

First Edition

*for you.*

The space between everything, all of it is love.

# GRATITUDE

WHEN I KISS MY HANDS TOGETHER TO PRAY, GRATITUDE MUST always come first. And I'm going to start with you. Thank you. Whoever you are, wherever you are in this life's iteration, I am grateful. Whether you found this book or this book found you, we are about to embark on this journey in tandem. This book comes alive with you, with your imagination. You are the life, the conduit, no matter the reaction. Thank you again—I love you. All of it is you.

To my family, I love you from the deepest bottom of my being, each and every one of you in your own special way. That has always been and will always be the driving force of any of my art—my acting, my writing, my shows, my paintings, my music, my marriage, my everything. All great art is troubled, painful, healing, ridiculous, and thought-provoking, all at the same time. And I promise you the worst things in this book are about myself, my deepest darkest secrets, my lowest points in my drug addiction and alcoholism and Hollywood, which led to my transformation, my transition, my healing. This book is a rebellion against the rigidity of standardized gender identity and an exploration of all the ways our current generation has evolved to express themselves when it comes to constructs of gender, sexuality, and love. Some of it focuses on my own programming and family dynamics. Fortunately, I have had each of you to help pave my way over the years in different ways.

Mommy, thank you for always holding space. You are the rock, even when you crumble. Thank you for believing in me, even when you couldn't see it. Thank you for supporting me, even when you didn't understand. To my stepdad, I see you, I respect you, I love you. My brother Rocco, I am here for you always, no matter what. To my parents and grandparents and siblings and aunts and uncles and cousins on all sides of the family, I am grateful for the space to call on you. All of it is you.

My lovers over the years, you know who you are. Thank you for showing me how to love, how to be loved. Arielle and Mary and Sarah and Bridget and Antoinette and Andrew and Jamie and Sara and Red and Emma and Lindsay and Gabriel and Kyle and Peter and Henry and Joey and La Démi and Olesya and Ian and Leyna and Johnny and the ones I left out and the ones I haven't met yet. All of it is you.

To my friends who carry me, I am beholden to your capacity to give grace. Eric, your story may not be in this book, but it is with me forever. Jean, Jean, Jean, I love you so much, you asshole. Alok, I will always spiritually bend a knee and bow to your abundance. The words "thank you" will never be enough for what you have shown me. To The Love Bomb, Will Malnati, thank you for trusting the work and propelling the message. Mitch and the rest of the team of At Will Media. To Milk and Paige and Eric and Sas and Ryan and Harvey and Lane and Bryan and Emily and Jules and Love and Colby and Jeremy and Coco and Breezy. To Courtney and Todrick and Hanne and Chad and Jennifer and Mickey and Sheila and Shaun and Jeaneane and John and Celeste and Jasriel and Patrick and Zeke and Tommy and Johnny and Rain and Lacey and Paul and Maryanne. To Gavin and Chris and Ronnie and Lisa and Jordan and Bianca and Emily and Elsz and Blair and Ivanka and Vic and Michelle and Shoshana. To Sutton and Debi and Molly and Hilary and Peter and Miriam and Darren and Joey and Nicole and Justina. All of it is you.

To my team, who I would be lost without. Steve, thank you for guiding the ship. Kyetey for seeing me. Bianca and Devin for believing in me. Eric and Ryan and Courtney for joining at this stage in the game. Laila for being a teammate no matter what. Tricia at Crown for creating this with me. Josh and Tennessee for lighting the way even in the darkest of times. Tennessee Jones, for real, this would not exist without you. Thank you for giving voice and validation where I couldn't. Celeste Fine for fighting for me. And Sarah Passick for constantly, no matter what, proving that a best friend is worth more than all of it. All of it is you.

To my wife, my husband, my best friend, muse, butthead, soul mate, twin flame. Bethany Christine Meyers Tortorella . . . baby, baby, baby, none of this matters without you. All of it has always been, all of it is you.

And to myself. I want to thank me. All of me. All of it is me. All of it is you.

*Please, universe, take care of me.*
*Angels and Gods and aliens, please help me.*
*I pray for myself and pray for my family,*
*My lovers and strangers and enemies,*
*Shine light on me so I can properly see,*
*be.*
*I pray in the name of love,*
*be*
*not this, not that, beyond definition.*
    —The Love Bomb

And thank you again.
I love you.
Amen.

'VE BEEN TRYING TO WRITE THIS BOOK FOR MONTHS NOW. AND I don't think it's an accident that it's finally coming as I sit here in my dream house. A sprawling chapelesque estate on thirty-three acres—thank you, *Younger*—about an hour and a half north of New York City, in this little town where I'm already starting to feel at home. I've been up here for days now, writing, writing, writing, going over every little detail of my life, all the joy, pain, and regret, while I pound the keys. You've heard of somatic manifestations, right? Where your body says "fuck you" because of all the stuff going on in your brain? Well, that's happening, proof that writing this book is a birth in its own right. I'm feeling the agony of delivery: debilitating lower back pain, contractions and muscle spasms that result in full-fledged panic attacks. I'm going over my past and some of it is ugly, but most of it is beautiful even in its flaws, and I'm giving birth to myself, right here and now, as I write.

Girl. Bro. For real. Just breathe.

What's wild is that as your dreams start coming true, you

start to dream different dreams. You start to dream bigger; you gain the ability to shift intention. You start to set aside the old shit, and opportunities to turn over a new leaf emerge. That's what healing is, right? Shedding an old skin as you grow into a new one, like a snake discarding its former shell as a natural function of survival. Through this creative process of healing, I've learned that I wasn't born into the wrong body. No, I was born into the wrong world. Realizing this is a big part of my story.

Today, press is rolling in from some of the recent activism I've been involved in—an NBC interview about the Trump administration's proposed anti-trans legislation, and a *People* article about a protest I had participated in the weekend prior for the advocacy to end intersex surgery. For as long as I can remember, this is all I've ever wanted. To use whatever fame I have for the purpose of justice, and to make a den in the middle of nowhere to raise a brood. These are my priorities: the ability to leverage a career to effect positive change, and being able to walk outside to kiss the earth and develop a symbiotic relationship with the land.

I'm in a back brace and have to lie on the floor to take a break, next to the fire blazing in the eight-foot hearth. I've thrown my back out before, but never quite like this. I thought it was maybe because I haven't been working out as much as I used to, or because I've been wearing heels a lot more than I did in the past, or because I took a fall mountain biking last week. Some combination of the three has led me to this. As I lie here staring into the flames, it hits me. The deeply profound lesson in all of this.

We hold our emotions in different parts of our body—our repressed emotional pains and deep hurt in our lower back and pelvic floor, our shoulders and stomach. The past four days I have purged the last thirty years of my life onto the living room walls, storyboarding this book with index cards, a black marker, and tape. At the same time, the country is gearing up for midterm elections and I have been actively pushing an agenda on social to *ride that blue wave*. All while some of the most incredible career validations have been unfolding for me. And the glory, trauma, and disturbance surrounding my childhood, gender, sexuality, career, and addiction resurface and manifest as this angelic vision. Me: a fucking mess. Though as I look around I am able to see the medicine.

The house is ornamented with religious iconography, childhood keepsakes that remind me of my family and of past lovers, and treasures from my travels. I can see my altar in the distance and crawl my way to it. My God, Gods, and angels. My spirit guides, my Patronus, my crystals and tarot cards and *palo santo* and dragon's blood and every other herb, image, candle, incense, and stereotypical pseudoscience ritual object I've collected over the years. And I pray. First there is gratitude. And then there is love.

By telling my story, I hope to give something back to you. Storytelling is art—the art of healing. I've known that since I was stage-acting in Chicago as a teenager. The craft, my first great love. As much as I still love this art form and will continue to pursue it, I'm more interested in telling my own story, in playing the most authentic version of myself, rather than retelling someone else's. Only then will I actually be able to give all of myself to the characters written for me. I have always believed I would never feel totally successful until I knew I was able to make an offering to the world. In the wake of the current administration's blatant attacks on trans, intersex, gender-nonconforming, and all-around human rights, I had to find a way to express myself in the best manner I know how. Through art. This is about y'all. This book is about all of us.

We are at the precipice of big changes toward love and inclusivity. The future is fluid. But so is the past. We as human beings have all always been fluid in some capacity, our journeys perpetually in motion, ready to bend and shift when necessary. It is precisely in that space between where the truth resides. The real magic. The self-actualization.

Splitting billions of people into only two categories—men and women—is maybe one of the most foolish things we've ever done as a human race. The great dichotomy of the world. It's no wonder we put so much pressure on the categorization of gay and straight and the binary constructs of masculine and feminine, and why the space between is so confusing for people to understand. We've been taught one thing in this country since the beginning. Well, two things. You are either "normal"—a straight white couple with two and a half kids and a white picket fence—or you are "other," by which I mean you're somewhat excluded from the category of "human" as it's constructed and enforced by mainstream culture. We are inherently afraid of what is unfamiliar and deemed "different." In our personal lives, we very much understand the gray areas of things, the spaces between, but it's much easier to tell a story if it is definitive. But we're not always definitive. We can say or believe one thing today and learn something tonight and then use our voices and actions to change tomorrow.

Through my own education about sexuality and the LGBTQIAPK+ (I know, so many letters) community at large, I have begun to break down the systematic construct of binary gender, male and female, and its propelling nature of "division." It is no secret that we are markedly divided, here in the United States and abroad. The binary pronouns *he* and *she* can be inherently divisive, which is one of the many reasons I have started using *they* as a pronoun for myself. Which hasn't been an easy conversation to navigate. Not with my friends, family, coworkers, or the media.

And when asked if my pronouns are plural, I say yes: I am a multidimensional dynamic human being.

We all are. My queer journey has shown me that gender is multivalent and continuous—not two opposing poles, but a nuanced spectrum along which we have the freedom to explore the space between. *This* is what I mean by gender fluidity.

But *they* as a singular pronoun has been used in the English language for a ridiculously long time. Shakespeare wrote using singular *they* pronouns—check out this line from *The Comedy of Errors*, act IV, scene 3:

> *There's not a man I meet but doth salute me*
> *As if I were their well-acquainted friend*

We refer to people as "they" on a regular basis. When a car cuts you off in traffic you might say something like, "They just fucking cut me off!" Though many people make a case against the use of the singular "they" because it's supposedly grammatically incorrect, its usage is a pretty normalized part of the English vernacular. So why is it so hard for people to understand "they" when it comes to gender-variant identity? Because of what we've been taught. You are either a boy or a girl. You are either straight or gay. You are either a Republican or a Democrat, conservative or liberal. Dichotomies. *They* as a singular pronoun cuts straight to the heart of the gender binary, and reveals it to be false.

In other words, it names the space between.

Today, seventy-one gender options are available on Facebook. Every day younger generations are rewriting terminology for identity and expression through the social media revolution, and I can't help but beam with pride. This isn't a new fad; this is the reawakening of what has always been.

While the language we use to describe ourselves is ever changing, gender-nonconforming people are not "new," nor are they a "trend." Historically, in every corner of the world, multiple genders have been recognized, celebrated, and worshiped by indigenous peoples. But because of colonialism and coercive religious indoctrination, alternative understandings of gender and sexuality have been demonized and erased.

We will not be erased. Not today, not yesterday, and certainly not in the future. Both sexuality and gender as we understand them today are recent constructs that I refuse to abide by. The scientific and biological facts are evident. The spiritual connection is abundantly clear. We are all kings. We are all queens. And I'll be damned if we aren't all the space between.

*Space Between* opens the opportunity for discussion to everyone inside and outside of the queer community, and offers a dive into the depths of our collective consciousness and universal human understanding. The philosophy of infinite love based on oneness that is propelling our lives—whether we realize it or not.

And what does *queer* even mean? As an umbrella term, *queer* can be used to mean anything other than heterosexual and cis—a word reclaimed in the modern world from its pejorative usage against people attracted to the same sex. I use it as a broader word to describe the ever-growing spectrum of non-normative expressions of gender and identity. I also see queerness as a form of resistance; for me, being queer inherently opposes the white-supremacist hetero-patriarchal capitalist system in which we are living. The experience of coming to understand the ways I've learned to hate myself because I'm queer has helped me to see how social constructs work to separate and harm all of us, in ways that are in service to people who already have material wealth and power.

Beyond a rebellion against the rigidity of standardized gender identity and an exploration of all the ways our current generations have evolved to express themselves when it comes to the constructs of gender and sexuality, this book is about the infinite singularity that unites us all, the all of us, the all of you. This book is about family, friendship, programming, fame, addiction, healing, and how the driving force is, has always been, and will forever be love.

I am aware that my programming is not like everyone else's—or even *anyone* else's. I fully acknowledge my privilege and the access it has given me to so many different people who have informed my education, and that I've learned to use my position to help lift other people's voices and make sure they are heard. My white privilege. My straight- and cis-passing privilege, the privilege of my overall appearance. My job, the celebrity, the characters I play on television, the money I make, where I was born, where I went to school, my primary relationship, all of that privilege. If you look up *privilege* in a dictionary, there might as well be a picture of me. So why does it feel like I'm fighting so hard to rid myself of these skins?

The answer is, I don't have a choice. Once the veil was pulled back, I could see the world for what it really is. I recognize the responsibility to use my power and privilege to speak for something so much greater than my own experience. This is about human rights. Gay rights, lesbian rights, bisexual rights, trans rights, women's rights, indigenous rights, brown and Black and migrant rights are just that—*human* rights. And if we're not speaking out for them, who will?

I'm an actor by trade, thespian at heart. Right now I'm on the show *Younger* and play a straight, cis dude named Josh. I have also played a bisexual serial killer on *The Following*, a jock who gets shot in the nuts by Ghostface in *Scream 4*, a drug addict, a DJ, and a handful of other somewhat normal straight dudes. It's my job as an actor to transform. It's my job to get the audience to believe I am the character on the screen. Why is it so important that I play a role offscreen as well?

When I was younger and just starting out in my acting career, I did plenty of interviews where I only spoke about my relationships with women, almost as a badge of honor. As in the rest of the world, in Tinseltown there are these unwritten rules and guidelines on what it means to be a leading man, or leading woman, for that matter, and I always knew that I wasn't following them. I was always asking myself: *Who am I supposed to be? What am I allowed to stand for? What do I have to hide about myself? How can I fit into the studio system's perfect little box and appeal to the mass market?* Why is it okay for actors to play gay roles but not okay for the actors to actually *be* gay? A "straight" actor plays a gay character (relatively problematic in this day and age) and people cheer because he's brave. Oscars for everyone! But where's the credit for the gay actor playing a superhero in a movie that pulls in a billion dollars at the box office? We owe it to that guy to be less hypocritical about gender. While we're at it, we also owe it to his female costar, who was paid 30 percent less than he was. We've got to be talking about this shit if we want it to change. I'm just trying to do my part.

Back in the day, if the studio didn't like your parents, they would just hire you new ones. And fake girlfriends and boyfriends were rolled out on the red carpet weekly. It's not quite that bad today, but it's no secret that PR bullshit like that still happens. Thankfully, I have a team that is very supportive of me. That doesn't mean I haven't spent hours deep in conversation with agents, managers, and publicists, discussing who I am supposed to be, what I am supposed to say and do, and what I should post on Instagram. But I'm at a point in my life—and I think we're at this point societally, too—where I can safely say: Fuck. That. Shit.

Most of my crazy-ass wonderful friends and lovers in the

queer community have labeled themselves something other than straight. Apparently, less than half the generation younger than me identifies as straight. *Yassss, kweeeens.* We are becoming the majority. So why are we still so groomed to act a certain way? Why have so many actors been closeted for so long? The answer is in these rules. *You need to walk like a man, talk like a man, spit like a man, fuck like a man. Don't ask, don't tell. Keep your business and personal lives separate.* Archaic limitations that I refused to stand by.

Sexuality has always been such a taboo, but through my personal education by the queer community at large, I've begun to deconstruct even the idea of binary gender, which has led to a much more complex understanding of sexuality. But for the average folk who only see the world through the lens allotted, we have some explaining to do.

While I prefer to state that there is fluidity to all of this and that nothing is fixed, if you still need a label to help process who I am in terms of my sexual and gender identity, I am comfortable today calling myself a queer, nonbinary, bisexual (or pansexual, depending on the social-context semantics), happily married, polyamorous/non-monogamous human being.

The more work I do on myself in regards to understanding just how complex sex, sexuality, gender identity, and love are, the more able I am to represent something that lives outside of myself. Which, in 2016, was the impetus for starting my own podcast, *The Love Bomb,* which ran for two years. We did forty-four episodes, in which I explored love and the labels associated with it. In each episode, I had a conversation with an individual about what love means to them. For me, it was a way to telegraph the conversations I was having in my waking life about the LGBTQ (those were all the letters I knew at that point) community. It was the moment I really started to take the conversations seriously, and to take them public. I have grown up in this community with all of you. But I'm still just a teenager (metaphorically, that is . . . I'm officially in my thirties); we have a lot more work to do. And I thought, *What better way than to give you all my own* Love Bomb, *my episode as a book?* I want to let everyone know exactly how I got to this point, in the hopes of fostering understanding and love.

Look, I haven't always been the greatest to people, but I'm trying to be better. And the truth of the matter is, I've been in some pretty toxic, emotionally abusive relationships over the years. And I have had some of the most incredible fairy-tale romance sagas anyone could ever dream of. In some cases, names of people involved have been changed, details altered, and stories combined in order to protect their anonymity. I wouldn't trade a single experience with any of these people for anything. I haven't always been the best to myself either, but I'm trying to be better.

I am beyond grateful to have had so many different people come into my life who have informed my perspective. My own queerness came into being not just from meeting other queers, but because everyone in my life, my family included, has been a queer figure to some degree. There is always something off-kilter about people. No one perfectly fits these tropes and archetypes we put on pedestals. And because of this, what I am most interested in is leveraging it all for the greater good.

I repeat: I am not in the wrong body—I am in the wrong

world. We all are. As much as we believe the system is broken, the system is working. Far too well. The matrix has been masterfully configured to keep us oppressed and silent while the 1 percent reaps all the benefits. A system built to make a select few successful while the rest of the world perishes. A system built to keep us apart. A system built to keep us down, dormant. A system that tells me that because I have a penis, I am not allowed to be feminine. A system that demands I destroy every feminine part of myself so I can adhere to the archaic patriarchal rules bestowed upon me and my ancestors, first by the church, then by colonial settlers (some of whom were my ancestors), then the government, then the media, then my parents, then my teachers, then my peers, then Hollywood.

But if success is what we were taught it is and the academic world is spitting out leaders, experts, and politicians with big plans to change everything, why is the world the way it is? Why are so many communities still so marginalized? Why are we born to this earth as equal spirits but immediately segregated into unequal bodies at birth?

As the sun is beginning to set and the geese are honking in the marsh, I sit in my living room and look at the index cards covering the walls, mapping out this book. Part of me is ready for this; part of me isn't. And in the space between, the book will begin to write itself. I am on—*we* are on—a feelings journey.

All of it, no matter what, is love.

# SPACE BETWEEN

## CHAPTER 1

MY NAME IS NICO TORTORELLA, SHORT FOR NICOLO LUIGI Tortorella—a real mouthful of prosciutto. Although my birth certificate says Louis, not Luigi, Mom's always said my middle name is Luigi. She wants to make sure everyone in the world knows we're Italian, but my grandma is the only one in the family who's actually set foot in Italy. Well, I went to Milan once for fashion week, but that doesn't really count. Someone I used to date once told me I'm about as Italian as the Olive Garden. But my mom definitely isn't having it when I try to correct her by saying we're Italian American. *Shut the fuck up, Nico, you're 100 percent Italian. Don't ever forget it.*

Nico is not a family name. My mom was eight months pregnant and watching the classic Hollywood film *Above the Law*, a story of a native Sicilian detective in the Chicago Police Department played by the one and only Steven Seagal. The Legend. (This was his first movie and pre-#MeToo.) His name in the movie was Nico Toscani.

Bam!

Between the ponytail, tinted glasses, and martial arts training, that was it: my mom had decided my name. I still like to believe she was really into the Velvet Underground in the seventies and named me after the real Nico of the century, but as the story goes, my mom was a disco queen and Steven Seagal was her one and only source of baby-name inspiration.

I moved out of my family's house in the northern Chicago suburbs when I was pretty young, only seventeen. The North Shore is about as white and privileged as you can get—if you've seen any John Hughes movies, then you've seen my high school. My best friends were some of the richest kids in the country, but my family lived on the other side of town. Our house was a pretty modest working-class kind of place that my parents had bought with my grandmother's help when they were still together.

The performing arts were taken very seriously at my giant school of four thousand students. Every year I was in at least three different choir classes and two acting classes, which took up most of my days. I guess I was what you might call a stoner intellectual artist thespian. There was some speculation about my sexuality in high school, but the theater department was insanely insular and provided an environment where it was socially acceptable for me to be relatively queer while still maintaining a veneer of heterosexual masculinity. Ever since high school, I have always been able to play this masculine heartthrob role while also being a flamboyant thespian, which I think is a foundational aspect of my gender—I can be on *Younger* and also one of the queens.

I took myself pretty seriously, but at the same time had a Ferris Bueller air about me; I took time to stop and look around and enjoy life, no matter how fast it was moving. And I always tried to make sense of my life through art—it really does have the power to alter reality. For instance, all the seniors at my high school had the option to take the last quarter off to do an elective thesis project of some sort. Most kids went off to do internships or philanthropic "life experience" expeditions that would look excellent on college applications or other typical upper-class, privileged activities. But somehow I persuaded my teachers that proper learning, for me, would be to construct a twelve-by-twelve-foot mixed-media mural in my garage (while smoking a ton of weed). My cousin lived across the street and helped me build the wooden structure on which to paint; it ended up weighing over four hundred pounds. I mapped out what I wanted the piece to look like on a small scale, and split that into sections before I started working on the real deal. I was always working on paintings and had even sold some, but this was my first large-scale endeavor.

I called the piece *Free Will*. It was a larger-than-life representation of Da Vinci's *Vitruvian Man*, split between the binary divides of the world—the physical and the spiritual, the city and the country, nature and nurture. Ever since I was a kid, I had been obsessed with positive thinking and the mystic writings of Ram Dass, Dan Millman, David Wolfe, Napoleon Hill, and other modern spiritual folk my aunt and uncle had introduced me to at a very young age. The mural had a geometric component to it, and running across the entire lower quarter was a metal fence that the charcoaled *Vitruvian Man* was reaching for, begging to cross over, desperate to reach the other side and be free.

I worked on the piece for six weeks, and it was truly fucking epic. We'd built it to fold in the middle so we could transport it, but still needed an eighteen-foot flatbed truck to move it to school. My mom had a guy (my mom always had a guy), and it took six of us to get it into the auditorium, where it towered above all the other exhibits. It was such a proud moment for me, standing in my high school for the last time with something substantial to show for my efforts.

At that point in my life, I was an actor through and through. Half my school days were filled with acting and choir classes, leaving no time for anything else. I'd been acting on the stage since middle school, but in the auditorium in that moment, I realized what I really wanted to do was make art that was a tactile and visual manifestation of my internal thoughts. Art as change. That mural was the beginning of something so much bigger than I realized at the time.

Once the presentation was over, I had to get that dude out of the auditorium and figure out what the hell to do with him. I couldn't take him home; I had nowhere to store a piece that colossal. I could have left him at school, but I couldn't bring myself to let someone else decide his fate. There was only one thing I could do—destroy him.

I hadn't seen or spoken to my real dad—I hate the way that sounds, excuse me—my *birth father* in a long time, but I knew he was the only person for the job. But before I tell you about the demolition, let's back up for a minute so I can tell you some more about Pops.

My mom and dad split when I was four and my little brother, Rocco, was two. My parents have kind of a hopeless romantic love story. My dad was already married and his first wife had just had a baby not long before the night he walked into my mom's bar, where she was making drinks behind the bar, being her beautiful, brash, Italian American self. If the story Mom tells is true, Pops never went back home after that.

The earliest memories I have of my daddy are from right before he and Mom divorced. Even now, it's like it was yesterday that I was standing between the two of them in the kitchen while they were arguing about God knows what. Actually, I do know: my grandma had just moved in with us. If you ask my dad, that's the real reason they split; they stopped sleeping in the same bedroom when Grandma started living with us. My brother and I had bunk beds in the room adjacent to the master bedroom, and there was a third bedroom, which was also an in-house tanning salon that doubled as a guest room. (Yes, my mother had a tanning bed in our working-class abode. Classic Mommy.) That room became my dad's bedroom, and though my brother and I usually slept with our mom and had literally since we came home from the hospital, I would sneak off to my dad's room as much as I could. I can still smell the perfumed concoction of coconut tanning lotion, beer, cigarettes, and distinct man musk that would fill my nose as I nestled my way into the crook of his arm to fall asleep. I loved it in there more than anything—the bedroom, the nook, the safety. I remember the day he left, the first time his bed was empty, never to be filled again—at least not in the same way.

If you were to ask my mom today why they got divorced, she would probably say something like, "I married your dad for the Italian last name and because he looked like Kurt Russell. I wanted beautiful Italian babies with Italian names, but I wanted a lifestyle he couldn't support. I wanted an upper-middle-class life instead of a working-class one, and that just wasn't your father." Her actual words would undoubtedly be a lot funnier and less PC.

It's true, what she says about Pops. He's never really cared about the material world or making more money than he already has. I mean, my dad was a garbage truck driver when we were really little. I remember him taking me to school in a garbage truck, and I thought it was the coolest thing ever. My mom says she's the one who actually got him that job; that she had to force him into going to the public works facility because he didn't have any drive of his own. I obviously don't take after him in that way, but my dad is a lover through and through, and I'm really thankful he gave that to me.

His love is truly unlike anything I've ever witnessed in a man. To this day, when I see him, which is not that often, he kisses me on the lips and the sting of Carmex reminds me of being a little kid. This dude is in love with Carmex. Whether it be his physical touch, the way he chokes up when saying good-byes or talking about the past, the way he smiles, the way he eats, drinks, smokes—this man just wants to be happy. Which is probably why the marriage had a few hard spots, especially after Grandma moved in. My dad and my grandma represent two opposite ends of the happiness spectrum; they were never meant to gel. It didn't help that Grandma moved in because her husband had just died. "Your grandma, the asshole," my dad still says. And he isn't wrong. She *is* an asshole. But I can't help but love her.

After Dad left our house, he moved into an apartment above a bar in the next town over. He had this bachelor pad–style place with a roommate, and then he met his third wife, and they had a kid, my little sister (love you, girl). A few years later, they moved to a town about an hour away. My dad still worked for the city in my school district, and sometimes I would meet him for foot-long Subway sandwiches with extra giardiniera at the Winnetka gazebo, where the ice rink scene from *Home Alone* was filmed. Over the years, though, we just kind of fell out of touch.

*Fell out of touch* . . . that's something we say about ex-lovers, not our parents. But once my dad left, I became very skilled at dissociating. In fact, I don't remember large chunks of my childhood due to the trauma surrounding his absence. My dad had a new wife and new kids, and he chose to prioritize his new life. It hurt that he was present but not present, that he was around but never there. Even though I still had my uncle and my stepdad as surrogate father figures, I still grieved the loss of my dad. That initial abandonment probably accounts for a lot of my pattern behavior, from dating to materialism to addiction. Missing him now, I am able to recognize the ways in which his leaving actually fed my queerness, fed my polyamory, fed my celebrity, fed my addictions.

I couldn't even remember the last time I'd spoken to my pops when I called him to help me demolish *Free Will*.

He showed up at school on a Friday with tools, and for a couple of hours we worked together to annihilate the massive piece of art I'd worked on constantly for the past six weeks. It was cathartic, meditative, painful. I felt happy and sad, all at the same time, as we took apart my art and put it in a Dumpster—especially doing it with my dad, who'd been gone for so long. It was so special that he was the one who came to the rescue, that he was the one who showed up to free my will, in one way or another.

I MOVED OUT later that summer to go to art school in Chicago. I spent my first couple of weeks in the dorms, sleeping on another fucking bunk bed, which really wasn't for me anymore, so I quickly found a loft apartment that my mom helped me pay for without my stepdad knowing. (Even when we couldn't afford something, she would always find a way to make sure I had the best of the best.) I started living on my own and was wicked excited to be away from my family and to put my focus into making art. I was a serious raw foodist and had been doing yoga since I was twelve. The yoga had started because I was diagnosed with a rare spinal disease and my physical therapist recommended yoga as a means of healing, but even after my spine healed, I didn't give it up. It kind of naturally went along with my other spiritual obsessions, which included a deep relationship to the earth, crystals and tarot, all things pseudoscience, conspiracy theories, and plant-based medicines—

aka smoking pot, eating mushrooms, and questioning exis-tence as we know it.

I was always interested in healing—healing myself and other people—and that was a big part of what I was doing when I was stage-acting in Chicago as a kid. Maybe I wasn't conscious of it then, but looking back, I think one of the things that drew me to studying the craft when I was in mid-dle school was the feeling that storytelling is a kind of healing art. They say the first step to recovering from any trauma is to tell the story, to bring it to a witness outside yourself. From early childhood, we construct our own personal narratives in order to make sense of our lives, and these are informed by what we are taught by the world around us. Our interpreta-tion of the stories we tell ourselves and one another has the power to shape who we become, teaching us what to do in the future and—maybe more important—what *not* to do. Learning to reframe these stories by telling them to others is one way we can stop negative patterns that harm ourselves and others, and also begin to see the ways in which our traumas not only stem from our highly personal experiences but also from the systems of domination and ideology that shape our respective worldviews. Being honest about our traumas is a way to get over the shame of being hurt, to heal from the ways in which we've been wounded, and to recognize how we've wounded others.

When I moved out, my grandma was still living in my mom's basement, running the antique store she'd had forever. When I was growing up, our basement was full of boxes on top of boxes overflowing with old lace and needlepoint and "As

Seen on TV" throwaways like the Big Mouth Billy Bass singing fish that seemed to always be begging to get thrown back in the water. There were antique dressers jam-packed with Victorian underwear and Edwardian matchbooks and tchotchkes and knickknack paddy whacks. And let's not forget the taxidermy. Deer, reptiles, birds—all kinds of shit that was both awesome and creepy. I'd spend hours rummaging through that basement daily, and those are some of my most treasured childhood memories. In addition to being an antiques dealer, my grandma is an estate sale expert extraordinaire, a garage sale gal, a collector—okay, she's a hoarder. Like, full blown. And that basement full of her shit was my personal playground.

I was the only grandson who took an interest in any of it. I used to go to auctions with her on the weekends. We would start bright and early in her minivan, singing along to the same Frank Sinatra cassette playing on repeat all day. Her voice was known throughout the entire country—not for her singing, but for her foul mouth. Her old lady cursing rivals that of the best of them. She grew up in Italy, the old country, and moved to New York when she was just a little girl. Her mother had died shortly after giving birth to her, and she was left to be raised by her father and older brothers, which is probably part of the reason she's such a hard-ass. Unfortunately, my grandma is a fucking racist homophobe, and she'll say and do pretty much anything. Now, I could go on and on about how her beliefs are generational, how it's what she was taught as an oppressed immigrant herself, but there's zero excuse for hate and ignorance. Still . . . oh my God, do I love her so much, no matter what. She's my Nana.

It wasn't just her, either. Race was a big thing in my house growing up. And by race, I mean racism. Full disclosure, the N-word was used on a regular basis—either the N-word, or *mulignan*, which roughly means "eggplant" in Sicilian dialect (I know). My family had a word to say about everyone who wasn't like us. Ninety-nine percent of the people I grew up with were white and predominantly Jewish, which my family had a lot to say about as well.

One of the first times I remember seeing my family's racism for what it was happened when one of the first Black families moved into our neighborhood. They had a son, Jamal, who struck me as queer, wound up being one of my best friends in sixth grade. We were really close, and my family freaked out on me when I brought him home. My mom and my grandma didn't want me hanging out with any Black kid, let alone this effeminate Black kid. One day, he and I were drawing in computer class, goofing off, and I drew earrings onto his ears with a marker. He was into it, like swooning and queening, and I was happy to have a male friend who wasn't a macho asshole. The next day, his parents came to school, and I got called into the office. They thought this white kid was bullying their son. Jamal and I weren't really allowed to hang out anymore, and his family left the district not long after. To this day, I find myself thinking about him; I would love to see him again.

Racism doesn't need to be conscious to still be racism. We are all raised in a given set of circumstances, often with certain prejudices, no matter where we come from. Now I know that what I took as normal was actually white supremacy. I'm ashamed of being complicit in my family's racism through my silence, but it's something I'm able to recognize now through my education and relationships with people of color. Discrimination is taught, yes, but so is consciousness. It's up to all of us to decide how much we are willing to accept, how willing we are to stand up to injustice. We can't go back and change the past, but we are responsible for our present and future.

Back in 2006, I wasn't as woke as I may be today, but I was beginning to wake up in my own right—well, at least in my own apartment. I went to Grandma's collection to find things to furnish it with. I took about a hundred records from the store and used them to line the walls right up to the ceiling. I collected all her religious and spiritual iconography, which made logical sense next to my giant Phish and Dave Matthews posters. Taxidermy on the walls, rugs on rugs on the carpeted floor. My own hoarding—I mean, collecting—had begun.

Before I ever knew exactly what an altar was, I had already set one up. I positioned a Muslim prayer rug with a clear picture of Mecca at the center of its red fringed wool in front of the altar. Cross-cultural, sometimes contradictory religious figures ordained the mesh shelving, always with the proper amount of *nag champa* burning. I was honoring all these archetypes without ever really knowing who or what they were or where they came from. But somehow, they helped me make sense of the reason I was even an *I* in the first place. Through thousands of years of reason and religious indoctrination, people were given spiritual purpose in their lives, which was something I was always striving for. I needed to know more, so one of the first classes I enrolled in at college was Theology 101. I was getting to know these symbols in and out of the classroom in all sorts of ways. And now that I had more space, I was going to fill it with meaning.

THIS BOOK IS a lot of things, not least of which is a love story. Love for myself, love for the world, and also, love for the person who will, by the end of this story, become my life partner. Bethany Meyers, my wife, my husband, my best friend, my partner, my everything. The little pixie who swept me off my feet with their all too familiar brash sensibility and undeniable grace. Their sense of style and their way with words. Their instinct and flamboyant impulsivity. Their love, their sense of self. Their sense of me.

When Bethany and I met in 2006, I was a boy and she was a girl, whatever that really means. Today, Bethany and I both identify as nonbinary and prefer *they/them* pronouns. Which is exactly how I will refer to them throughout the book, as a way to normalize this simple language and help people feel honored, represented, comfortable. Although people get tripped up over these descriptors being plural and therefore grammatically incorrect when used as singular pronouns, *they/them* are actually very fitting descriptors, given that we are all multidimensional dynamic beings. We use pronouns to reflect our gender identities, so it makes sense that these plural signifiers contain more than two options. More than the binary.

I met Bethany at a party in college just days after I moved

to downtown Chicago. The connection between us was instant, electric, even, but Bethany made sure to tell me right from the get-go that they had a pretty serious boyfriend and couldn't ever imagine themselves with anyone else. Bethany left the party before anything could happen between us, but we lived in the same building and our paths would continue to cross.

A few nights later, Bethany came over to my apartment with a few girls, and I pulled out one of the treasures I'd taken from Grandma: a wooden trunk I'd upholstered and painted with pagan symbols, which now housed the wine and weed. I was the only kid on the floor who had a bong, so the party commenced. Bethany wound up staying later than everyone else, and we talked late into the night about religion and programming, getting high and drinking Two-Buck Chuck.

Bethany was the first person I'd ever started having feelings for whose upbringing was entirely different from mine, and that difference played a big part in bringing us so close together so fast. They were from a super-conservative Baptist family in southern Missouri, and all the mixed religious iconography in my room was sinful, to say the least. They grew up believing in the Rapture—like, one day they'd just be driving down the road with their parents when the Rapture hits, and if they hadn't accepted Jesus Christ as their Lord and Savior, their family would just disappear and they would be left behind. Bethany also didn't believe in evolution, and had learned from their family and church that there's no such thing as self-determination. As in, God has already written down everything we're going to be in His Big Book. I mean, if that's true, then what's the point of doing anything, right? They grew up as one of those kids who would knock on your door on a Saturday morning, Bible in hand, and ask if you knew whether you were going to heaven or hell. I was captivated, leaning into every word with bated breath, wanting to know as much as possible.

That whole night, I knew something was going to happen between us at any moment—we both did. And it probably would have, if Bethany hadn't suddenly gotten off the couch and left without even saying good-bye. They still had that boyfriend.

Maybe a week later, I was passed out in my room around two a.m., when someone started pounding on the door like a maniac. There was a wild thunderstorm happening outside, pouring rain and big flashes of lightning piercing the sky. I opened the door, and there was Bethany standing in the hallway, soaked through with rain. "I broke up with my boyfriend" was the first thing they said.

And then it happened. Straight out of a classic rom-com in slo-mo. Lips taking a full minute playing games with each other, getting closer and closer until they made love. Wet clothes flying off. Laughs and sighs and almost tears. Cue the soundtrack. Bethany and I have one song, our song: "Blessed to Be a Witness" by Ben Harper. And my god, was I blessed to be a witness to their being that night. The thunder rolled, the lightning struck, and, yes, we both came, to witness, to actively participate in the soul storm.

So, buzzkill, I stopped seeing Bethany after only two weeks—don't ask me why. I think I was probably freaked out by having met my match, my twin flame, if you will. I mean, I was really just a kid, and even though I had all these high-minded spiritual ideals, I think I was just too young to handle any of it. Later, Bethany would say they knew I wasn't ready for commitment, but who really is at that age? And even though we'd only spent a couple of weeks together, Bethany remembers looking at me and thinking, *Nico's gonna be in my life forever.*

Who knows if it was good fortune or free will, but just a couple of months later, Bethany and I encountered each other again when some friends of ours threw a proper party for underage kids called . . . wait for it . . . Soul Storm. They had this idea for a dramatic flyer of a man and a woman, all dressed in white, kissing each other in the middle of a snowstorm. Obviously, Bethany and I were their top choices to pose for the photo. We showed up to the shoot separately, and for over an hour, we were standing in the middle of a room, fans blowing fake snow around us, our lips almost, almost, almost touching all over again. I felt like our bodies were magnetic, voltaic, even, two people as one flame eternally. That day, I came to my senses—it had been insane to break up with them in the first place—and after that, it was game on. Bethany's upbringing also taught them something super fucked-up about being gay. When they were a kid, they'd asked their Bible school teacher why anyone would choose to be gay. The teacher explained to them that God made people gay as a punishment for being particularly bad, evil sinners. It would be years before Bethany told me that the night of the Soul Storm party was the first time they had ever felt attracted to a woman. Bethany said they were watching this girl all night, not at all sure what they felt, but when they saw the girl making out with a guy, they suddenly knew: they wanted to be the one kissing her, felt jealous that she was kissing a boy instead. But Bethany didn't know what to do with these feelings because they weren't supposed to be having them. Did that mean that *they* were bad or evil?

One of the greatest things about talking to Bethany was having to really explain my beliefs, which contradicted almost everything they'd been taught was true. Having experienced an entirely different spiritual upbringing, I had to dig deep to explain them in a way that made sense. I took Bethany to their first yoga class, something they'd always been taught was weird and maybe even satanic, and they also started getting into raw food and meditation with me. Both of us were changing fast, and I started to finally admit to myself that there was something big going on between us, something real, but also something unspeakable.

We'd been seeing each other for a couple of months when something completely unexplainable, beyond magical, went down. It was December in wintry-ass Chicago, and it was freezing outside. My apartment was just one big room, and I'd put my mattress in the walk-in closet because that seemed like the most logical place for it, if I wanted to have a little privacy when I had people over. I know that's a little on the nose, all things considered, but whatever: It wouldn't be the last time I'd have sex in an actual closet. Or the last time I'd come out of a metaphorical one.

In that windowless container bedroom, miraculous events

unfolded between Bethany and me: we were not even touching each other, but our spirits combined, and it was like nothing I'd ever felt before—I don't know that I have felt it since. Our energies dancing, doing something harmonious, symmetrical, and erotic all at the same time. I know some of you are rolling your eyes, some of you are googling "energy sex," but some of you may understand. At that point neither of us knew what was happening, just that it was new and beautiful and beyond any orgasm we'd ever imagined. Tantric. Kundalini awoken. Bodies basically levitating. It was the most religious experience either of us had ever had.

Afterward, I called my aunt and uncle to explain what had happened and to ask my uncle (who was, for lack of a better word, my guru when I was growing up) what it was and what it meant. I was my uncle's chosen one, his favorite. He was a professional judo champion back in the day, a real man's man, with a soft side that is a mystery to anyone who has had the pleasure of meeting him. This is the person who told me from day one that he was the smartest man in the world and would give me all the secrets to life, no joke. My aunt and uncle were the ones who really bred my alternative being—I was the kid who went vegan in fifth grade because his aunt and uncle told him to. So whenever I had a question about anything otherworldly, my aunt and uncle were who I called. And I needed help deciphering what had just transpired between Bethany and me.

Yes, maybe it sounds a little weird to call your family about something like this. But my uncle and aunt were the ones who turned me on to the teachings of spiritual healers, raw food, yoga, and crystals. They did more than just give me books to read and take me to lectures. They demanded greatness in my individuality, told me I was capable of anything and everything as long as I believed it to be true. They gave me a sense of self, sometimes to a fault.

Some of my greatest memories ever from being a little kid are of my aunt and uncle coming over for Christmas. They always showed up after we'd eaten—mind you, they were hardcore raw vegans and disgusted with the standard American diet, or SAD, as they called it. "You are what you eat, my boy!" I can still hear him saying that to me on a daily basis. Side note: My relationship with food has been rocky over the past thirty years, but I'm no longer burdened by the religious constraints of a specific diet—the food binary: *this is good, this is bad.* Rather than *You are what you eat*, I say, *You are what you believe, my people.*

So they would show up after our sorry holiday meal with $100 worth of singles for each of us. Real Italian *Godfather* stuff. Then the family would commence playing poker around the table until someone finally won and got to keep the entire pot. I always had the spot to the right of the dealer, which was always my uncle, of course. Sometimes these games moved past the cards to Secret Santa–style envelopes with surprises inside that they had brought for the whole brood—a large amount of money, a car, a Doberman (they had six), or something else grandiose—but sometimes, it was Jack Shit, literally. I remember pulling an envelope that read "Jack Shit" one year and thinking, *Who is this Jack guy, anyway? And is he happier than everyone else because he doesn't need anything?*

Bethany came over for Christmas the first year we were dating. I was so excited for them to meet my infamous aunt and uncle. They'd already talked on the phone and hit it off, and my aunt and uncle had even written us these beautiful letters, describing everyone in the family as a piece of fruit: I was a young coconut, my mom was a watermelon, Rocco a kiwi, Grandma a durian, and Bethany was a lychee, this delicate, perfect, tough-skinned fruit that ran with clear, sweet juice. When Bethany saw the letter, they said, "Does this mean I'm part of the family now?"

But Bethany was pretty shocked when they actually encountered my family for the first time: we talk to one another like we don't give a fuck. Everything is super direct—you never have to wonder what someone's thinking about you because they've already told you—unlike other families, where you're always wondering how they're judging you because they're obviously doing it. So when my grandma looked at me and yelled, "You look like a little bitch lady," because my hair was too long and I'd lost some weight, and I told her to go fuck herself in return, Bethany knew they weren't in Missouri anymore.

As it would turn out, that was the last Christmas my aunt and uncle ever spent with us. The next year, they split for Florida, just left the entire family behind without explanation. More family abandonment trauma for me—bring on the daddy issues! I'm being glib to avoid feeling the pain of them leaving us—leaving *me*—without explanation. But fuck that, it was traumatic and it further solidified my lack of trust in men, specifically, because my uncle was always the one who made the decisions. I had lost not only my family—I had lost my teachers. And it would be ten years before I'd even try to heal things with them.

THAT MARCH, Bethany and I went to Mexico for spring break. This was the first time we'd ever gone on a trip together—they fully had to lie to their mom about it—and the first time we'd ever had real time alone, away from our friends and families. All we had was each other, the sun, a new country and a new language, and our willingness to adventure. It was an all-inclusive resort, and Mexico is one of those places where the drinking age is younger than twenty-one, so Bethany and I were pounding all the tequila we could get our hands on. We were still teenagers, day drunk on the beach, and we spotted this couple, a lot older than us, probably in their forties, who were visibly different from all the other people at the resort. We could just tell they were cool, very French, fucking hot—most definitely not normal—and we wanted to know more.

I was very attracted to both of them, especially him. He was this hot European daddy, but I knew better in that moment than to direct my attention toward him in front of Bethany. This would be our first experience having group sex, and I'm not sure either of us was ready for it. While I was conscious of my queerness to some degree, desiring him and not acting on my feelings spoke volumes on how much more I needed to grow. Timing is everything.

One night the four of us ended up getting drunk together, smoked a joint, and sauntered our way up to our suite. There were two different showers in this huge bathroom, the kind surrounded by glass, out in the open. Bethany and the guy were on one side, and I was with the woman on the other. A heteronormative swinger split. So as Bethany was hooking up with the guy, bodies slammed to the glass, steam a-blazing, I could see what was going on. And it was not what I had expected—I had this feeling, not of jealousy, but like I was missing them. In that moment, a deep sense of loving them took over. I ended up not being able to get it up.

Okay, now would be a good time to tell everyone I've sometimes had issues getting it up over the years. And it can be the most embarrassing thing for all parties involved, but it doesn't have to be. Energetically there is something way deeper going on there, and it doesn't have to do with being with a girl or a boy, or being straight or gay, because for me, it's happened with both. And it's happened to a lot of people I know, but no one really talks about it; no one even talks about taking the blue pill prescribed to make everything better. (Fucking Western medicine.) Having a rock-solid hard-on is what makes you a man, right? False. Years later, after therapy and developing a deep spiritual understanding, I've come to terms with this being caused not by any sort of physical factor, but instead by psychological factors like guilt, fear, addiction, and depression. And I'm not ashamed of it at all. Some humans with vaginas fake orgasms, some humans with dicks can't always get bazooka hard. Maybe it's our bodies' way of telling us we shouldn't actually be doing this. Like an energetic protective warning. I like to think that I haven't even hit my real sexual peak yet.

Anyway, I woke up the next morning feeling ashamed; I

had a guilt hangover on top of everything else. Bethany and I talked, and they told me they had felt jealous while everything was happening. We'd wanted to experiment, and we had, but neither of us was emotionally ready for it. It would be a long time before we tried anything like that again. I tell this story now because, looking back, it was foundational to the merging of our queerness. That night I remember really thinking about the differences between "male" and "female" bodies in terms of attraction and performance, and the shame I felt about not being "man enough" to perform.

When we went back to Chicago after that, Bethany and I got a lot closer, and now I wonder, *Was that time in Mexico our first queer experience?* Even though I didn't sleep with the man and Bethany didn't sleep with the woman, we all wound up in one bed on top of one another, which made it feel undeniably queer. Or have *all* our experiences been queer, even though we didn't really know it—or couldn't admit it—yet?

I have been wondering, at what point does someone "become" queer? I don't think you can really draw a line in the sand. It's like that possibility is already in us, before anyone acts on the impulse. Looking back, I can see the signs of my emerging queerness; I knew something was always different about me ever since I was a kid, even though I didn't have the language to describe it. My earliest memory of this innate queer sense has a lot to do with my stepdad.

Shortly after my dad left, my mom married my stepdad, whom she met through her niece who worked at the Mercantile Exchange in Chicago. He was an amazing father to Rocco and me when we were little kids; still is. He'd been a state champion competitive power lifter, and some of my earliest memories are of him throwing me and my brother around the house like it was nothing. He's a man of few words, but when he's got something to say, you listen. I don't want to say he was homophobic, but slurs and jabs were thrown around in jest. I doubt he's ever been outwardly violent toward anyone, but words have a way of building up without anyone realizing the long-term ramifications. I grew up in a house full of that type of rhetoric, and even made those jokes myself until I realized what they actually meant. This behavior—this hate—is passed down from generation to generation, and it only ever changes when someone stands up and takes a stance against it. Hearing all that homophobic bullshit from my family definitely warped my perspective of what was considered acceptable.

While my stepdad is not gay, it's funny how the most hypermasculine guys are often the ones who engage in the most homoerotic behavior. Football players slapping each other's asses, talking about dicks, or, in my stepdad's case, having copies of *International Male* sent to the house. Now, if you know what *International Male* is, you feel me. But if you don't, let me give you a little insight. *International Male* was a men's catalog that existed from 1974 to 2007 and was especially geared toward the dandy. As a competitive power lifter, my stepdad had the body to show for it, and he liked wearing clothing that accentuated it. But let's be honest here: these catalogs were basically soft-core gay porn. There was a separate insert in each catalog called UnderGear. It was dicks on dicks on dicks on jockstraps on bathing suits on dicks. And it was always in the drawer next to the toilet in the bathroom. Needless to say, I always knew when the new issue came in.

The tension between my stepdad's hypermasculinity and hearing all those homophobic things around the house, and then knowing I *needed* to look at those catalogs he ordered confused me. Now I realize that even presumably straight cis men can have elements of queerness. I can't tell you the number of times over the years seemingly straight dudes have hit on me, saying, *I'm not gay or bi, but if I were, it would be you . . .* All masculinity inherently has this kind of homosociality at its core. And part of my sexual energy has always been geared toward appealing to people who aren't queer. What are you supposed to do with that kind of crazy mixed messaging?

The summer before I moved to Chicago, I hooked up with a guy for the first time. We were friends, but not super close. We had gone out one night in the city and wound up taking a cab back to his house in the suburbs, since his parents were out of town. I remember kissing him for the first time and feeling his stubble on my face and knowing—it felt right. Although I was many sheets to the wind, it is the one sexual experience from high school I remember the most. Our bodies just fit together. Skin on skin. Body hair on body hair. Sweat on sweat. It was something more primal than what I had experienced with women up to that point.

We woke up the next morning and talked a lot about what had happened and what it meant moving forward. I remember having a discussion about not defining ourselves by who we sleep with but rather who we sleep as. I played it cool. He drove me home and I went to the basement to shower. As the steam enveloped my barely pubescent skin, I cried. I knew I'd talked a big game with him, but it had been a very, very big deal for me. I wish I could say that I didn't feel dirty, but I did. I wish I could say that I didn't feel like I had done something wrong, but I did. Deep down, I knew it wasn't, but there was this pain that demanded I actually feel what had just happened based on society's standards, rather than just play it off as this not so important moment in my sexual development.

For so many queer people, there's no going back after their first same-sex experience. But I wasn't ready to fully embrace my queerness; I still had things to figure out. I told my best friends in high school that I was maybe bisexual, but I didn't tell Bethany about this experience until years later. It's not like I was necessarily hiding it from them; I just didn't talk about it because I didn't have the emotional understanding of what it all meant. But Bethany and I talked about everything, so why didn't I tell them this? Why did it take so many years? I guess I kept it to myself because it was something that was *mine*. My sexuality. My gender. And I only discussed it with the people closest to me when I felt comfortable enough, and on my terms. Perhaps this was because I felt shame about the experience, which is a natural reaction to our collective conditioning when exploring the ranges of our desires, but sometimes only from shame can someone begin to own their truest desires. My utopian dream would be that no one ever has to feel any sort of guilt whatsoever surrounding their sexuality or gender. But that's not the world we live in yet. I guess this is a big part of why I'm telling this story in the first place.

I KNOW IT sounds crazy, but when Bethany and I were together in college, we were kind of holding each other at arm's length, not really admitting our feelings. We would be at parties, talking to other people, across the room from each other, and strangers would come up to us and be like, "Hey, what's going on between you two?" Even the first time we said "I love you" was super casual. It was sometime after Christmas, and I just said, "Hey, you know I love you, right?" They said, "Yup, I love you, too." And that was it. After Mexico, things were different. We were closer, more of a couple, and we started being upfront about the way we felt about each other.

I had only signed a short lease on my apartment, and it was coming to an end, so I decided to shack up with Bethany for a few months. It was never supposed to be a "baby, let's move in together" kind of thing, but there we were, living in sin. I'd already decided to change schools, and the next fall I'd be moving to LA to get an MBA at Loyola Marymount. Me, in business school, y'all! Art school to business school—genius idea, Tortorella. Growing up, I always knew I'd find my way to Hollywood somehow, and that was apparently the easiest way to convince my mom. So it seemed like our relationship might have an expiration date. But there are a couple more stories I want to tell you about us and how we tried to figure ourselves out alongside each other before I moved.

That summer, before I left, I took a sewing class. I had always had an obsession with fashion and form, and I was getting more interested in sustainable material, so I thought I'd see what a pattern class was all about and learn how to make my own clothes. I made a dress for Bethany (it was too small for me), this beautiful flowing white muslin thing, and surprised them with it at our apartment. I pulled out the trunk of vices and we blasted Brandi Carlile while dancing through our neon-painted kitchen. I threw a belt on it, put on an outfit to match, and we frolicked through the apartment, both feminine, both in love, both free. Bethany remembers that night as being magic, and it was. So many parts of my life got wrapped up in putting that dress on them, the process of constructing it, constructing the night. Looking back, that may have been our first wedding night. Believe me, we've had thousands. And as they modeled the dress in our apartment, I adorned them with all my grandma's costume jewelry from the store.

Like I've said, my grandma is a raging homophobe, to the point where even though I was the only one interested in all her vintage stuff, she wouldn't let me take anything feminine. If I picked up a woman's bracelet or ring or flowing piece of cloth, she'd take it away from me. "Put that down, that's a lady's! You're not a fucking lady! People will think you're a queer!" But when Bethany was with me, we could take anything. All I had to do was point out what I wanted, and Bethany would pretend it was for them. Queer bandits. My grandma hasn't changed over the years, and this charade is something Bethany and I still do when we visit. She's never given a fuck when Bethany picks up something "masculine." It's always a bigger stigma when "men" dress or act feminine. This is yet another way misogyny expresses itself, just in case you needed an additional example of how the patriarchy is fucking you.

When I was a little kid, my mom used to let my brother and me help her with her makeup, hair, and jewelry when she was getting ready to go out or to work at the bar. We would blast some Diana Ross and parade around the house wearing different furs while she had rollers in her hair, chasing her with lipstick. When she came home late at night, I would help take off her makeup by delicately picking the mascara out of the corners of her eyes. And when she slept next to me, I would twirl my fingers in her hair to keep her next to me as long as possible after I fell asleep. I guess the makeup routine stopped after I got a little older, probably around the time I hit puberty. I mean, my mom would never want to raise a sissy.

For me, this wasn't one of those instances of a boy in a dress putting on his mom's lipstick only to realize he was different. I never felt like I was in the wrong body. And the more I realized I had been born into the wrong world, not the wrong body, the more things started to make sense. I didn't feel more like myself playing dress-up or more like myself masquerading around the house in heels with the Supremes playing in the background. No, I always felt like myself. I feel like myself in boy's clothes, I feel like myself in girl's clothes, I feel like myself in all clothes. I struggle with the idea of gendering clothing in any way whatsoever—I mean, it's actually ridiculous, when you think about it—but I would be lying if I said stereotypical masculine and feminine clothing didn't play a huge part in my understanding of myself. I feel like myself when I'm having sex with a person who has a vagina or with a person who has a penis. With a person who has body hair or a person who was taught to remove it. All of it is me. And that's part of the queer experience that isn't always celebrated or even talked about. Maybe we don't have to feel uncomfortable with who we are, or feel shame in order to become who we're really meant to be. And maybe that's a privilege, but is it one allotted to each and every one of us if we choose to raise our consciousness?

My gender and my sexuality are not defined by what I wear, or even whom I'm sleeping with at any given point. They are defined by who I am. Which is something that is constantly changing as I critique myself and grow as a person. Every new thing I learn changes who I am and how I understand my place in the world. This is my fluidity, this is my space between. It's a way to work within socially constructed ideas about "men" and "women," and express how I actually *feel* inside to find ways to be true to myself. We are all working with the hetero-patriarchal ideas of gender we've received through conditioning, but this doesn't mean we can't queer the fuck out of them.

Rather than there being one defining moment when I realized I was queer, it was more like a bunch of small things that accumulated over the years. Ironically, the realization came from an array of unlikely sources—like my family, whose homophobic rhetoric ultimately pushed me away from heterosexuality, even though that was the last thing they wanted for me. They don't seem to recognize the roles they played in my personal development. So, sorry, Mom. Maybe you didn't get a "man."

But you did get *me*.

## CHAPTER 2

BODY ART HAS ALWAYS BEEN VERY IMPORTANT TO ME, AS YET AN-other vehicle for storytelling. My older cousins all have tattoos, so it seemed like a family tradition—a ritual, even a rite of passage. My mom took me to get my first tattoo when I was sixteen, which is proof that she really is cool as shit. Unfortunately, I was a culturally uneducated white stoner suburban kid, and got three-inch-tall Chinese *hanzi* in the middle of my upper back. They were supposed to read, "health, wealth, and happiness." Fortunately, I quickly realized how fucked up this cultural appropriation was, and right before I left for LA, I got another tattoo to help cover them, or at least distract from them. Bethany came with me, and we ended up having our first real fight, caused by jealousy.

A couple of weeks earlier, I'd flown to LA to check out an apartment I'd found on Craigslist. I had posted an ad looking for a roommate who understood the vibes—spirituality, conscious manifestation, 420 friendly. This girl responded pretty quickly, and she and I immediately hit it off online. When I flew to LA to visit Loyola Marymount, I drove up to Santa Barbara to meet her. Her family's house was this sprawling estate situated among rose gardens, and as I entered the living room, above the fireplace, I saw that she had a large painted portrait of Ram Dass. *Be Here Now* was my absolute favorite book at the time, and Ram Dass was a personal hero. As it turned out, he was this girl's *godfather*. I've always had a crazy kind of luck, where things just seem to fall into place and all aspects of my life somehow resonate. I don't really believe in coincidence; I believe in synchronicity. We're all so connected, in one way or another, and everything that happens is like a symbiotic butterfly effect. I went back to Chicago even more convinced that LA was going to be the right place for me. It was as if the universe were holding me, rocking me back and forth, validating every single emotion I had been feeling. I had a major transition ahead, and I needed all the help I could get.

All the art I was doing in school was element-based. Earth, fire, water, air. I had this theory gifted to me in a dream that the stars and planets themselves were plants grown by a higher spirit. I was painting and drawing the earth, sun, and moon as foliage, and was obsessed with the idea of plants as medicine, as spirit, as things that grow and die and grow again. Life birthed from a seed of knowledge. From seed to feed. The tattoo I decided to get to take attention away from the ill-chosen *hanzi* was an iteration of this idea: two plants with roots on either side of the characters. The left, my feminine, sprouted the earth and moon. The right, my masculine, the sun and an orchid. I was subtly flipping gender constructs even before I had the appropriate language to do so. The tattoo was to mark my transition of moving from the Midwest to the land of sun and stars. And because it was on my back, it could push me forward.

Bethany and I went to Cherry Bomb Tattoo in the Wicker Park neighborhood of Chicago to see an artist who had tattooed my cousin the year prior. I knew he was the perfect guy to nail the bold art I had created and to execute the delicate watercolor all at the same time. While I was getting the tattoo, a bunch of texts from the girl in LA came in, and since I was lying facedown/ass up, I asked Bethany to grab my phone. As they read the stream of texts, they couldn't quite believe nothing was going on between me and the girl and stormed out while I was in the middle of getting the tattoo.

When I got home, Bethany was sulking in the bedroom, and I quietly approached and wrapped my arms around them. Over the years I've become very aware of when Bethany needs comfort and when they need me to stay away. Whenever we have an argument, I always have to be the first one to break the tension, and I'm okay with that. No matter what, it's always my job to make it better. And it *was* getting better, even if I was leaving.

There really was nothing going on between me and this girl, and we worked all that jealousy out pretty easily; we've always loved a deep, intimate conversation. We understood that tensions were high because so much had happened between us so fast, yet we had this expiration date. In later years, after life demanded change, Bethany talked to me about the jealousy they'd felt—or "adopted," the word they used—over the years. Like, it wasn't their true self, but they had to dig down through layers and layers, the years of patriarchal programming, being taught one man/one woman, happily ever after, to learn that. Jealousy is a normal human emotion, but to think you have the right to dictate what someone else does with their body—that's conditioning. It's another version of ownership. Another way capitalism digs down into our hearts and bodies and commodifies even our most intimate relationships.

In so many ways, that's a huge part of what our journey has been about: learning that loving someone doesn't mean you get to say who they love or what they do. You don't get to say who they are *becoming*. Really loving someone means you get to be a witness, blessed to be a part of their experiences, even if only sometimes. It means that no matter what they want or need, you allow space for them to have it, and anything they want is cool, because you love them. Unconditionally. And when you come from a place of release, of finally letting go of what you think a relationship is supposed to look like—this idea of "mine"—that's when you really reclaim yourself, too.

MY BROTHER ROCCO, my Wook (that's my nickname for him since forever), helped me move to LA before classes started at Loyola Marymount. He and I had already been through a lot together—he was the only other person in the world who could understand growing up in our mom and stepdad's house. I don't know what I would've done without him. My stepdad, in addition to having a subscription to *International Male*, also had two big-ass Dobermans, trained to kill, death bites to the jugular. Don't get me wrong, I loved those dogs more than anything, but they were no joke. He used to hire people, without telling us, to break into the house in the middle of the night to help train the dogs. You can't make this shit up, am I right?

Rocco is twenty-one months younger than I am, and our mom used to dress us exactly the same growing up—matching striped onesies, matching leather jackets, matching earrings, matching everything. Like me, he was a hockey player, and he's done some acting, too, but he never fully transitioned to make that his career. Rocco's knees and shoulders are both totally shot from playing hockey. They used to call him The Enforcer on the ice, trained to kill. Sound familiar? His senior year in high school he suffered a knee injury after getting checked from behind, and that led to him going on a long journey through addiction. But out in LA, he was pretty much sober, wild and high on life, which is the way he's always been . . . minus the sobriety.

Wook is magic. Pure unadulterated magic that has always manifested in abundance. My little brother is hungry for life, eager to go beyond his own limits. Even now, he speaks to me in waking life, and in our dreams, in a different language. We were like twins when we were kids—we knew what the other was thinking, and we created our own language. He was the kind of kid who would say some shit in the middle of a conversation like, "Hey, imagine if a dolphin just crashed through the ceiling right now." And then everyone would stop for a second and just consider that wild-ass possibility before telling him to shut up. If you're going to put your imagination in a box, Wook is going to make you at least think about what you're doing.

Wook sparkles—it's what he does. I've always believed that he could set the world on fire if only he knew how to strike the goddamn match. But his matchbook got wet, maybe around the time of the hockey injury, or maybe before that—I'm not sure. In my family, Wook has always been "Nico's little brother," always in the wings at my symphony, which isn't how I ever wanted it. All Wook ever wanted to do was protect me; this little boy who would turn into a father figure when I was climbing a tree because he was afraid I would get hurt if I didn't pay attention. My brother is a sorcerer who loves deeper than most people, and between us, that love flushes out reason and runs even deeper than blood. Which also means it's harder to clean up. Maybe his love is why the flame hasn't struck yet, why the matches are still wet. Wook, at one point, was the empath of all empaths, and it's hard to live in this world feeling so many things, imagining how things could go down differently. If an empath doesn't do the work to protect themselves from all that they feel, eventually they'll go mad.

Rocco and I both grew up in our mom's bar. By the time we were born, my family owned a few bars and an Italian deli. My family's origin story as immigrants in the United States has its roots in alcohol. When my grandpa first set foot in this country, expecting it to be the best place ever, he quickly discovered that Italians were treated like shit. Alcohol became a numbing agent, and somehow, he saw it as the means to a better life once he began profiting off it. He still is very much a staple figurehead in my family, even after his passing. The details surrounding his death are still somewhat of a mystery, but one thing is clear: he was an alcoholic.

Now, these bars were nothing fancy, just your run-of-the-mill local taverns where everyone knows your name. Our mom is the youngest of three, and she's always been the life of the party. According to Grandma, she was always Daddy's best friend and Mommy's worst nightmare. I believe it. I could actually write an entire book about our mom—her stories are epic. She used to tell us about driving cross-country with her boyfriends, dropping purple tabs of acid along the way. Or getting so high on speed when she was still living at home that she would iron not only all of Grandpa's clothes, but all the dollar bills in his wallet. When I asked her what kind of speed she was taking, she said, "Oh, the fucking diet pills your grandma was giving me."

When she was seventeen, the drinking age was still eighteen, but right before her birthday it changed to twenty-one. So she convinced her guy (my mom still has a guy for *everything*) who worked at Lutheran General Hospital in the shipping and receiving department to give her a box of blank birth certificates. She ink-stamped a bunch of them with a fake footprint, using the side of her fist and fingerprints to dot the toes, then proceeded to hand out new fake IDs to all her friends. I mean, my mom is *extreme*, and so are Rocco and I.

Mom smoked cigarettes, but this is one of the few things she hid from us, and if we ever smelled smoke on her she'd blame one of the middle-aged white-guy regulars who hung out at the bar. Guys with names like Peaches, Paul, Nuts and

Bolts, or Sarge. I loved those guys and saw them pretty much every day. I was serving shots as a little kid and felt as close to these regulars as I did to some of my family. The bar was vacation, and the people were loose. There was a bedroom downstairs where we would sleep sometimes and go to school the next day. There were pool tables and arcade games and an antique wooden bar about forty feet long. There were hundreds of trophies in the front windows that I loved cleaning. The walls were plastered with photo collages of all the patrons over the years. I can still smell the cigarettes burning inside and the cocktail of bleach and booze from the wet-mopped floors. I can still hear the jukebox blasting some of my mom's favorite disco.

The bar was where I truly got to know my mom. I'd spend days just sitting at the bar watching her interact effortlessly with the regulars and complete strangers alike. This was a place where people had fun, and that's exactly what we all did when we were there. A bubble of supposed freedom. And Mom taught us how to take advantage of every minute of it. My mom and I were best friends; my mom and Rocco were mother and son. Always have been. He was—*is*—her baby.

So Rocco and I got to LA, and in a surprising turn of events, I wound up not moving in with Ram Dass's goddaughter. My mom got into an argument with the girl's mom about the rent, and that was that. So there we were in LA, with no place to go, and I had to find an apartment. I was too young to rent a car, but I could rent a U-Haul. (Makes perfect sense, right?) I found a place in Playa del Rey (Mom helped with the rent) and lived all by myself. I've always loved living alone; it gives me space to truly create. I didn't know a single person in LA, and because I wasn't living on campus, I also wasn't really hanging out with any of the other kids at school. Shit, I didn't even know where I could find any weed. Although since it was Los Angeles, I knew it couldn't be too hard.

I went to this raw food restaurant called Juliano's RAW to try to get a job. Juliano was the king of raw food on the West Coast at that time. He was basically a celebrity to me, and I was obsessed with him.

As I mentioned, my aunt and uncle had been vegan raw foodists for thirty years, and they used to take me to seminars in Chicago about health, society, politics, and food. Afterward my uncle would assign me book readings to do and journal entries to write, which he would then look over and we would discuss. I was vegan in middle school, and all my school projects were related to animal cruelty and the evils of industrial food production. Middle school was also when I started getting into theater and stopped playing hockey, and suddenly all my popular jock guy friends started making fun of me for being a faggot theater kid.

Growing up I only ever heard words like *gay* and *faggot* used pejoratively. So it makes sense that my innate, God-given queerness was actually hidden under layers and layers of oppression. At some point we as a society became okay with calling someone a faggot, just accepted it as totally normal behavior. But maybe we're all actually a lot queerer than we think; we've just been taught to hate parts of ourselves and other people. It sucked to have my best friends turn on me like that, but my solution was simple. In the time-honored tradition of faggots everywhere, I just picked up and moved my social life to hanging out pretty much only with girls. I went from eating lunch with the popular boys to sitting with the popular girls, and let me tell you, I wasn't mad about it. Sometimes fortune works in mysterious ways . . .

In 2005, I became a raw vegan, which basically means eating only uncooked fruit, vegetables, nuts, and seeds. You know, rabbit food. Or as my uncle would say, gorilla food. I was a senior in high school and loved thinking of myself as slightly superior to all my peers, even if my mom did start getting phone calls from teachers about my new eating disorder. I also started journaling in earnest the day I went raw, instead of just sporadically. My uncle used to say that one day, after I'd won enough Oscars and directed or produced my own shows and movies, maybe I'd want to tell the story of my life. "If you journal now," he told me, "then maybe that book will just write itself." And, for sure, Uncle, you may not be the smartest man in the world like you've always said you were, but this is one of the things you were actually right about.

Anyway, meeting Juliano was a trip for me, and I walked out of there that day with the job. I probably thought at the time that it was all due to my impassioned speech about my belief in and commitment to raw foods, or my custom vanity license plates that literally read RAWFOOD, but in retrospect, getting hired on the spot probably had just as much to do with my symmetrical face.

My time at the restaurant changed my life in a couple of very important ways. One was that even though Juliano was straight, he dressed super-femme and androgynous. He had long flowing hair that he usually put up in butterfly clips, and wore dresses and bright colors and prints. I'd never seen a straight guy act like that, with no fucks given, and it gave me permission to explore my own appearance. I started wearing flowing clothes and doing all kinds of femme things with my hair, which was already hippie long. Now I can see that Juliano was the first nonbinary person I ever came in contact with.

The second important thing that happened at Juliano's was that I met Jamie, a redheaded Scorpio. Oh, Jamie. She's a true love of mine, one that just can't be categorized—maybe like every love, each one completely its own. The first interaction we ever had was in a yoga class she taught at her house in Santa Monica. She was training to be a teacher and invited everyone from the restaurant. As she was adjusting me in pigeon pose, I asked her to push harder. She looked at me and said, "So you're a sensation junkie . . ." And as those piercing hazel eyes met mine, I knew she really saw me. Jamie also had the weed. We wound up spending a lot of time together, skateboarding through Santa Monica and down by the boardwalk. Fully like teenagers falling for each other without a care in the world. Jamie was twelve years older than me (the same age difference between my character on *Younger*, Josh, and his love interest, Liza), but I don't know that either of us really thought about the age difference. I mean, we thought about it, but we didn't give it any weight. We just clicked. We lived in our own world; nothing else existed. She was into all the same spiritual stuff as me—meditation, plant medicine, yoga. She introduced me to Kundalini yoga, which is a practice to awaken the primal energy located at the base of our spines. And let me tell you, we awoke.

After our first trip together, both in the literal sense and the psychedelic sense (we loved eating mushrooms together), we never spent a day apart. It was like our souls were immediately magnetized. We mutually decided it would be the best idea if I moved into her house, and within a week we were shacked up. Now, I know what you're thinking: *new girlfriend.* Nope, at least not in the way you might imagine. This was a different type of romance blossoming. Jamie was in the process of breaking off an engagement right when we met. She wasn't trying to jump into another romantic relationship right away. We slept in the same bed for six months without ever having sex. We never even kissed till one drunk night in Vegas.

Sleeping in the same bed with Jamie was the first non-sexual physical intimacy I'd ever experienced. (Okay, fine, we eventually started jerking off together, but it was separate. Like we knew we needed the release anyway, and it was something we could do as friends.) In that bed was actually the first time I ever put anything up my ass, too. Are you ready for this? It was a spoon. Jamie was super into oil pulling, an ancient way of cleaning your mouth. So next to the bed was a jar of coconut oil and a spoon, and we thought, *Why not?* Prostate play is a real thing. Don't worry, the spoon had a very smooth, curved handle, and it wasn't the actual spoon end, you sicko. No judgment, though; do you. And yes, we washed the spoon and got a new one for the coconut oil, but let's just be clear . . .

we all put genitals in our mouths and most of us eat ass. So calm down.

We spent a lot of time together outside of the city, going to places like Big Sur, Ojai, and Anza-Borrego, and doing mushrooms and MDMA, constantly talking about our experiences of expanding consciousness. We fell in love, nontraditionally—our relationship was beyond platonic, beyond romantic. Jamie immediately became my family. It was like she was my best friend, my lover, my mother, my sister, and my greatest cheerleader all at once. For a while with Jamie, it was like I was getting deeper into everything I'd ever believed in, before things started to change. Before *I* started to change. I truly believe it was Jamie's orientation toward the spiritual that made her so cool with me dressing up in feminine clothing and frolicking around the house. She loved it (but always gave me shit for it in the cutest, most annoying way possible), and I felt totally safe to express myself however I wanted with her. This wouldn't be the case with most of the women in my life.

Jamie asked me if I was gay, all the time. Other than my best friend in high school, she was the only person in my life who'd asked me that point-blank. Well, my uncle did ask me once when I was in middle school when all the kids started calling me gay. He told me that *some holes were innies and some holes were outies* and that we weren't supposed to put stuff in our outies. And that was that. (The smartest man in the world, y'all.) I didn't tell my best friend or my uncle yes, because I didn't think I was. I wonder how many times people have to ask if you're gay before you start to think, *Maybe I am?* But, more to the point—the real point—why is *gay* the umbrella term for different? *Are you gay? Are you a lesbian?* That's what people ask if they smell difference on you. No one asks if you're nonbinary or trans, or if you're comfortable in your skin. You ultimately get reduced to who you're having sex with. No one ever says, "Hey, who are *you*? What do you believe in? What do you care about?" These are questions that might actually get us somewhere, but instead the focus is on what we do with what's between our legs.

I had my magic in full force when I met Jamie, my red-headed Scorpio, and then that started to change. Little by little, so slowly that I didn't realize at the time that it was happening. I wasn't making enough money at Juliano's—I had to work too much and school was demanding—so I got myself an interview at Ford Models. They had an open call once a week, and I walked in casual as fuck, but with high expectations. I walked out with a four-year contract. I thought I was making real money with that job. But, as it would turn out, I had no idea then what real money was yet. This is when my life started to take a hard left turn away from the spirit, toward the material.

There I was, a newly signed model, hair in an updo with twenty-six butterfly clips and maybe a dread or two (I know), wearing flowy draped floral-print frocks, high on life and love, living and breathing spirituality, traveling most of California in a car on the weekends with this fiery-ass Goddess, and still taking business classes at a Jesuit university. *One of these things is not like the others.* Since I had just signed this big fancy new contract, I had just enough fuel to convince my mother I should be working, not wasting my time in school. So I dropped out.

Jamie made it all better, made it all make sense. As my greatest cheerleader, she demanded that I recognize my full potential. She would talk to my mom on the phone and tell her I was going to make it and that she had nothing to worry about. When my family came to visit me, she took us all out to dinner and was emotional in relaying the magic of this *it factor* I had that she had never seen in anyone else, ever. I can safely say that if it weren't for Jamie, I wouldn't be where I am today.

One of my first modeling gigs was a Manson-family-themed, acid-'70s photo shoot at a mansion in the Hollywood Hills. For the shoot, I was wearing Victorian garb, flowy lace and a top hat, which was basically what I was wearing in my everyday life at the time. I met a woman there who had a tattoo on her arm that read *I love Charlie.* "Who's Charlie?" I asked, like it was an ex-boyfriend and I wanted the tea. She goes, "Charlie's for Charles. Charles Manson." Oh. *That* Charlie. Los Angeles is a weird fucking place, man.

I met my very first fairy god-gay on that shoot. Jean was an older, somewhat conservative, hard-ass magic gay man with fragile mannerisms who became a mentor to me. When he showed up to the shoot, I was immediately captivated by his walk, which somehow reminded me of both Clint Eastwood and Judy Garland. Jean immediately became my chosen family. It seemed as if we've been connected for eons. I love this man deeply. He is the real deal, whatever that means.

Jean was raised to believe that what he saw on the silver

screen was the truth. He likes classic structured beauty, and only certain images of Hollywood fit that part. As Carroll Baker said while playing Jean Harlow, "I wanted it to be beautiful and it was so ugly." He can't look at the ocean without thinking of Joan Crawford in *Humoresque*. Her beauty, her demise, and her freedom. These are the types of icons Jean started teaching me about. And Jean himself is a walking hyperbole in the most fantastical ways. A throwback gay who'd survived the plague near the end of the century, he was also obsessed with new Hollywood starlets like Paris Hilton, Lindsay Lohan, and Hilary Duff. But not in the same way everyone else was. He saw timeless qualities in them that reminded him of different eras. As a good fairy god-gay, he taught me queer history and theory using fancy storytelling rooted in personal experience. He knew Hollywood from the lost era, when studios would manufacture individualism and own everything, when there was no room for stars to be themselves. He warned me of the system's power of seduction. Jean has been sober from alcohol for the last twenty years, but will still smoke a joint or take a pill from time to time. He was the first person to show me that even sobriety could be fluid.

I wouldn't be the person I am today without him.

Since I was working as a model and wasn't going to school, it only made sense that I go back to my original love, so I started going on acting auditions. Jamie and I would rehearse for hours on end before auditions while feasting on avocado and bee pollen salads (God, do I love that girl). Luck was with me, and I very quickly booked a gig on a Nickelodeon show, playing a supporting character of the kid next door. They rewrote the character to fit my appearance, and in the pilot, the first time you see this kid, he's on the front lawn, doing yoga in all his long-haired glory. But the show didn't get picked up—something I got very familiar with over the years—which was a huge disappointment. All I wanted to do was work.

I hired a new manager, and he immediately sat me down. "Look," he said, "if you want to get real parts—real leading-man parts—you're going to have to look the part."

"What do you mean?" I asked.

"I mean you have the most beautiful skin I've ever seen, but the fucking hair has got to go. Get rid of it, and you'll start working."

The next day, I cut my hair.

My hair was everything to me. An extension of who I was. My lion's mane. They say hair holds memories, and I had started growing mine out right when I moved out of my parents' house. It was all I knew of my adult life, and I had been told to cut it. But I knew I had to work and that's all I wanted to do. It was numbing and pragmatic all at the same time. I had to prove to myself, my family, my friends, Jamie, Jean, and Bethany that I could do this. It was my first real tangible experience with selling out; there were many more to follow.

THROUGHOUT ALL OF THIS, Bethany and I stayed in close contact. I was still going back to Chicago a bunch for the holidays and always made time for us. Bethany had always dreamed of the California sun, as I had, and since I was already establishing ground out west, I asked Bethany to come. And they did—

Bethany moved to LA in the summer of 2008, about a year after I had. They had just graduated college with a degree in marketing and wanted to come to LA to pursue a career in sustainability advertising with a green company. They had been practicing yoga for over a year and were eating raw foods, and my twin flame came to build the fire in tandem. And they still were my best friend, no matter what. They knew I was living with Jamie at the time, but I'd never really told them about sleeping in the same bed with her—I just didn't know how to qualify that relationship, so I never tried, not until years later. Bethany and I had never referred to each other as boyfriend and girlfriend. We never really put a label on things between us at all, and I think that's part of how we've been together over the last thirteen years, even when we've been apart. Even now that we're married, we harmoniously resist.

When Bethany moved to LA, it seemed only natural that we'd live together, and that's what we did; we were already so good at the whole cohabitating thing. We moved to downtown Hollywood, the boulevard paved in stars, and I started to meet some of the Hollywood types Jean had warned me about. With Jamie, I'd been living on the west side by the beach, far removed from Hollywood proper. Jamie wasn't mad about Bethany and me starting over, but she definitely wasn't happy. It was only when I moved out that she began to see my age. She had known me only in the context of our bubble. And Bethany and I started going to clubs and partying more than we ever had, which was something Jamie and I never did (at least not in public). It wasn't Jamie's scene, and now she saw me as the twenty-year-old I was. Some of the people Bethany and I met around then were deep in the shit, but we were too young to know that. From our point of view, it looked like everyone was just having fun. And we were some of the beautiful people who got to have fun with them. Since I'd never had the real college experience, my partying years were still going strong.

Our physical expressions began to mark our transition to this newfound lifestyle. Bethany's and my fashion really started changing. We went from being these kind of hippie'd-out stoner-looking kids to dressing super dapper. Like, 1950s rockabilly-style, with minks and hats and two-toned shoes. As our inward energies were shifting, so were our identities. We went out a lot, but sometimes we'd get in the car and just drive. Up on Mulholland, where you can see the entire city, breathing in the night. Or we'd drive out of the city, to the woods or the desert, and camp, just the two of us, lying on our backs and looking up at way more stars than we'd ever seen in Chicago. I had met the rest of California with Jamie, and it was time to introduce it to Bethany. They had never really spent time in nature, and that time really allowed us to get closer to each other and me to get a lot closer to myself. Having had a little taste of success and luck with modeling and then easily booking the Nickelodeon show, even though it got canceled, was quickly changing my priorities. More and more, I wanted to get famous, something I hadn't thought about since high school. I craved celebrity in all its wicked forms.

In Hollywood, I was starting to confuse narcissism with loving myself. That's just the way the industry is built. The competition, constantly getting told, "No, you're too skinny/too fat/too young/too old/too pretty/too feminine" over and over again, breeds self-obsession, self-centeredness, and self-deprecation all at the same time.

But when Bethany and I took those long drives or went camping, with just us and the stars and nature, it was easier to touch the real core of me, the part that had been there since I was a little kid. Bethany has always been that grounding force for me. It's a huge part of our relationship. Looking back, that time we spent in LA, when we weren't at the clubs, was the only time we had a little taste of what we have now. We began to create the life I had always wanted, the vision of the future I had always imagined, of a house in the middle of nowhere and a partner to really make it a home.

Who knows how I would have turned out if my aunt and uncle hadn't turned me on to all the stuff they did, but I think it's safe to say that one of the reasons I took to their spiritual outlook on things was because it was already in me. From the time I was a little kid, I was hearing voices, seeing ghosts and visions. I would be terrified to walk upstairs alone because I would feel someone behind me. I was having full-blown conversations with spirits and worked in some of the most haunted theaters in Chicago. I saw apparitions and things that to this day I don't know how to explain. I think kids are more sensitive to the supernatural, and though I'd try to tell my mom and grandma about them, they wouldn't listen. They told me flat out that something was wrong with me, and if it continued, they would take me to the crazy doctor. They both looked down on anything you couldn't see or touch—no interest in the intangible—which is maybe one of the reasons my grandma's lifelong mantra seems to be *DENY, DENY, DENY!*

After all, you can't touch an emotion and you can't really put a price tag on it, either.

One of my grandma's favorite things in the entire world is her gold. She has enough of it in vaults to send all the grandchildren to college and then some (she didn't). And as her grandchildren, we were all given our fair share. When each one of us was born, she gave us gaudy guido bracelets she'd made with our names in diamonds, and as we grew up, she always made sure to remind us how much they'd cost and who had given them to us. Actually, maybe her favorite thing in the world isn't gold; it's always telling everyone that her hand is the hand that feeds. She used to give us hundred-dollar bills with handwritten notes in permanent marker professing her love to us, while also assuring us that something bad would happen if we spent the money. We've always known that Grandma is the one who made our family by working three jobs and never losing sight of what's truly important: money. It's a lesson my mom learned very well.

Given my family's obsession with the material, they didn't like that I had a connection with the paranormal. They didn't like having this kid running through the house saying there were ghosts creeping around and shit. And because I was a little kid, I was forced to listen to them, so I stopped talking about things I could see and hear that they couldn't. My grandma has an opinion about everything, and when anyone doesn't like what she has to say, her response is, "This is love. This is tough love. Deal with it." So I dealt with it, and by the time I was eleven or twelve, I'd made it so I stopped being able to see and feel those things. I *DENIED, DENIED, DENIED* them, and though I'm sure I was still tapped into the spirit world, I pushed it way underground to a place where it wouldn't bother me.

Of course, there's an irony to my grandma being so hard-line about this stuff. For instance, back when I was still playing hockey, she'd always rub Hostess Sno Balls onto the glass during the game. Sno Balls were good luck, she claimed. And while she was conjuring good luck for us, she'd be screaming profanities at the other team. The real reason she came to the games, I think, wasn't just to cheer us on, but to curse our competitors with the *malocchio*, otherwise known as the evil eye.

There are all kinds of stories in my family about my grandmother cursing people. But even today, you can't get a straight answer out of her about it. One minute she'll claim she doesn't know what the hell you're talking about. An hour later, she'll say, out of nowhere, "Oh yeah, my father killed a few people who crossed him with the curse." Of course he did.

One story in particular about my grandma and her witchy ways really sealed the deal for me. I first got hooked on acting when my mom made Rocco and me audition for *The Wizard of Oz* at the local children's community theater because she wanted us to be more extroverted. I got cast as a Munchkin, and from then on, I was in love. I performed in a handful of children's productions before I got a taste of professional Chicago theater: *Guys and Dolls, Oklahoma!, Oliver!, The King and I.* But the first big-time show I got cast in was a play called *Over the Tavern,* when I was in the eighth grade. It's about a Polish Catholic family in the 1950s with four kids—three boys and a girl—who live over a tavern that they own. (This whole "life imitating art" thing has really followed me throughout my career.) I got cast as the understudy for the two younger boys. The plot centered on the youngest and his questioning of the church. The middle brother was mentally disabled, and the eldest brother was sex-crazed.

The play started its run at the Northlight Theatre in Skokie, Illinois, not far from where I lived. It was a solid eight-shows-a-week schedule. The real deal. Our principal even booked a field trip for the entire class to come see a Wednesday matinee of the play. Again, I was an understudy, so if one of the two actors I was covering got sick or couldn't perform, I got to step in. The teachers knew I likely wasn't going to be performing, but booked the field trip on the off chance that I might.

Every night the month before the field trip I would go downstairs to the basement, where my grandma lived, to hang out with the Wicked Witch of the South of Italy. She would close her eyes and spit-chant in Sicilian dialect, all while making the sign of the horns with her hands. She said she was conjuring a sickness on one of the young actors so I could take the stage when my classmates came to visit.

And it fucking worked.

I got to the theater that Wednesday ready for whatever she might have conjured up. As I approached the green room, I saw Bobby, the actor who played the lead kid role, curled up on the couch in agonizing pain. Minutes later, he began to projectile vomit, and it was very clear that my time to shine had come.

I wound up doing that show for three years and played all

three brothers in different theaters all around Chicagoland—more than five hundred shows, my first real professional work. The joke at the time was that one day I'd come back to play the dad. Or at this point, maybe the mom.

I'd be lying if I said I wasn't beyond excited to get the chance to perform for my entire class, including all those jock dudes who had exiled me from their friend group when I chose the thespian path. In their eyes, I was officially the gay kid because I lived onstage, and I wasn't even sure I understood what that meant. But that day, a big part of me still felt scared and guilty. What else had my grandma cooked up for us over the years? (And why can't she use her magic for good and cast a spell that makes her not racist and homophobic?)

But when she laughs, I forget it all. When I remember painting her toes as a little kid, it feels like a memory of two girlfriends having a slumber party, rather than any sort of grandma-grandson relationship. When I remember her storming into my elementary school in her nightgown and rollers and cursing out my first-grade teacher, Ms. Trout, who had punished me for saying, "Oh my God," I remember who this woman is: an angel who forgets she has wings. A widow, a motherless daughter, an immigrant, a product of world wars and the industrial revolution, a pre-internet dinosaur riddled with self-doubt and self-deprecation and enough courage to run the underworld, who still believes the entire world is out to get us.

When I look down at the tattoo of her face I got on my left forearm a few years ago, I remember that the flaws she sees in society and her children and her children's children are a direct reflection of what she sees in herself. When I see her face on my arm, smiling, I realize I am literally bringing a piece of her to every situation I experience, the queer and anti-racist moments included. Somehow I'm including her in spaces she would normally disdain. And I remember how much I love her. No matter what.

Grandma, if you're reading this, I hope you don't hate this book as much as I have a feeling you will. And I hope you're proud of me even if you don't understand why.

*DENY, DENY, DENY.* Right?


BETHANY AND I were having a golden time in LA, even as I was starting to lose myself a little, that fame bug having bitten me hard. About eight months into our sweet time together, I landed my first serious job, as a series regular on the CW's *The Beautiful Life.* This was my big break, and it meant I had to leave LA—the pilot episode was filming in Montreal. Bethany was understandably hurt and pissed, but at the same time understood I had to go. They have always wanted what is best for me first, and for us second. Over the years I have had to miss out on birthdays and holidays because of work, and as much as Bethany wishes it weren't the case, they've always understood that the nature of my job is that plans can change in an instant. Vacations get cut short, family time abbreviated, and Bethany knew this. Bethany has always been wise and kind enough to accept these circumstances just as they are.

When I booked the new show, I couldn't take Bethany with me, at least not yet. I had to go play the game, and there was only room for one player. We were going off on our own paths, and my career had become more important to me than anything. Even just getting the call that I'd gotten the job was like mainlining something I wasn't ready to handle at twenty years old.

## CHAPTER 3

FELL IN LOVE WITH THE BIG SCREEN WHEN I WAS GROWING UP. *The Mighty Ducks*, and *D2* specifically, pretty much shaped my entire childhood and solidified my dreams of transitioning from hockey player to actor. (It's the only franchise besides *The Godfather* where the sequel was better than the original.) *The Parent Trap* and *It Takes Two* were family favorites. And then there were the stars. The Lindsay Lohans and Olsen Twins of the world. TV was another favorite escape, watching Nickelodeon and Disney and dreaming of what it would be like to be on *All That*. I looked so much like Ryan Merriman from Disney Channel original movies like *The Luck of the Irish* and *Smart House* that a woman stopped me in an elevator once in high school and asked if I was him. Obviously I wasn't, but she proceeded to tell me I could be his body double. I looked her square in the eyes and told her, "Nah, one day he could be mine."

TV was my window to the world outside what I knew, what I was taught. It was where I first found queer counterculture.

I remember the first time I saw two men holding hands on MTV's *The Real World: Chicago*, and quick, deep emotion coursed through my being. I also remember bingeing *Queer as Folk* in the basement late at night when everyone was upstairs sleeping, making sure to delete the evidence from the "recently watched" queue, knowing that I would get in trouble if my mom knew I was watching it. I found myself constantly repressing anything other than what was expected of me as The Straight Dude.

I dated a number of aspiring actresses early in my career, but for the purposes of this narrative I've decided to group them together as one singular archetype and call the composite character "Starlet," even though each one of them was a wildly different, beautiful individual. Some details, timelines, and accounts have been altered to maintain their anonymity. I have nothing bad to say about any of the people I've fallen in love with over the years. I have nothing but everlasting love, gratitude, and admiration for all of them. They helped shape the person I am today, and also the person I am not.

Hollywood is a difficult place for anyone to navigate, especially women in the industry. That's just how our manically patriarchal society operates. Women always have it harder, and still get paid less. And the competition for roles can lead to body dysphoria and hyper-low self-esteem. Actors in general are some of the most insecure people I've ever met in my life. And because of the patriarchy, women and trans people have it worse. But don't they everywhere?

Landing a role on *The Beautiful Life* was the first time I had booked a job as a series regular, and it was my hour to shine.

My art outside of acting had begun to manifest as a more tactile expression. I bought an antique sewing machine from the late 1800s, one of those heavy-duty steel Singers that was strong enough to punch through leather. I was making these incredible recycled animal-skin saddle bags with intricate embroidery and repurposed crystal jewelry. In the months before the pilot shoot, I made tons of trinkets to wear as ornamental armor. Bags and vests and necklaces, all with a personal signature touch. Very much curating the Nico Tortorella everyone was going to meet.

At the airport in Montreal, while waiting in line at customs, I spotted a Gucci purse sitting on top of Louis Vuitton luggage that just *reeked* of success. I looked up and recognized the star of the show. We locked eyes, gave each other's lavish accoutrements the once-over—store bought versus homemade—and immediately began sizing each other up. My gold-obsessed Italian family has a fierce materialistic streak running through it, and designer labels, furs, and diamonds were all part of the Hollywood fantasy. And Starlet looked the part.

This job was the real fantasy coming to life. We had women like Sara Paxton, Mischa Barton, and Elle fucking Macpherson owning the set. I remember the first time I met Mischa in hair and makeup and she was complaining about being hungry wickedly early in the morning. My mother taught me well, so I immediately jumped up and walked to craft service to grab her a croissant and coffee. Some people saw it as genuine, some saw it as opportunistic—a running theme of how I've been perceived throughout my career. Whatever. I've always known my intentions are pure and my heart is in the right place, no matter the haters back then or now. Nonetheless, it was clear that the women ran the show on this set, and Starlet had this confident ease about her that intrigued me.

She had that timeless Hollywood quality Jean had talked about: the platinum-blond hair, the perfectly symmetrical face, the girl-next-door vulnerability and the instinct to work that quality to her advantage. She also had an interesting thing going on with her gender, a masculine undercurrent running beneath the glossy image, which I really liked. Her physicality had this fluid air. The ability to shift at the drop of a hat from hyper femme to hyper masc. She was goofy, over-the-top, one of those women who could throw down like a bro. The type who wakes up without shame or guilt after a night of partying, something I was never great at, and could start all over again the next day. On the second or third night of the shoot, Starlet and I were leaving a party in someone's hotel room, and we went to give each other a hug good night in the hallway. It was one of those hugs that lasted just a couple of seconds too long—and I thought, *Oh shit, here we go . . .* Our cheeks against each other's, and then the *eyes*—peering into each other's with this childlike enthusiasm. It was on.

The Montreal shoot only lasted for a couple of weeks, and instead of flying right back to LA, the boys from the show and I flew to Costa Rica. *Pura vida,* baby. We spent a week in Central America, all while Bethany was gearing up to move out of our apartment in Los Angeles. We had started to grow apart. If you ask Bethany, we'd been on the same page in college and in LA, but when I left town and started acting like a movie star (by which I mean, an asshole), Bethany started to peace out.

We were in touch some, but I never told them about Starlet or the parties. I didn't need to; Bethany knew. And they knew they wanted out. Over the years, Bethany and I have honed our ability to watch the other take flight and, in one way or another, know the migration is important for self-growth no matter how much it hurt. This wouldn't be a forever separation, but a temporary and necessary one. One of my favorite things about Bethany is their ability to pick up and make shit happen, no matter the circumstances. They have a level of spontaneity and freedom that always seems to work in their favor, even in the darkest of times.

SO, THINGS STARTED happening *fast* around this time, really fast. Everything snowballed. While I was in Costa Rica, just after filming the pilot for *The Beautiful Life*, I booked a role in a Joel Schumacher film called *Twelve*. Joel has a reputation for making young kids into stars, and I had no reason to think it would be any different for me.

Shooting began in New York almost immediately, and I moved there for two months, living in a sublet at Thirteenth Street and First Avenue. I had only ever visited the city once before, when I was in middle school. I was ready to take a decent bite of the apple now. It was one of the most magical summers of my life. There is an undeniable reason it's known as the greatest city in the world. This was my first major movie, as it was for most of the young actors on the film. We were just kids, all the same age, working and partying together, owning the world. I was doing everything I'd ever wanted.

A few of us wound up getting really close. There was a boy and a girl in the movie, and we immediately formed a bond that I can't help but beam with absolute soulful joy when I think about. One night we got pretty fucked up at a party and wound up all hooking up in the bathroom, pretty innocently and pretty straight. Two boys in young love with one Starlet. This was my first real polyamorous "situation-ship," no matter how short-lived. We would spend days in her apartment in Soho, writing poetry, blasting music, making short films, and just being free. She went out of town one weekend and he and I stayed at my apartment for two days painting hot-air balloons and romantic verse on this door we had found on the street in the East Village. When she got back in town on Monday morning, it was pouring rain outside and he and I wrapped the door in garbage bags and walked it to her apartment to surprise her with it as a present. Fucking magic. In my life, rain has always had the power to cleanse, to clear the way for new experience. One night in early spring, this ridiculous thunderstorm came through and we left the apartment, stripped down to basically nothing, and ran through the streets downtown, laughing and high on life as the water blasted us. It was the most free I had ever felt in my entire life up to that point. That was the moment I officially fell in love with New York City.

RIGHT AROUND THIS TIME, Jamie moved to NYC. She'd grown up there, so it was a homecoming of sorts for her. We started spending a good amount of time together again and decided to get matching tattoos to symbolize the love we had shared over the years. Jamie had a magic number that I had adopted—39. 39, 3+3+3 = 9. Trinity. Sacred divinity. It represented knowing and trusting that everything is possible, that all is meant to be and all will be as it should be, that we are 100 percent taken care of and that nothing can go wrong. A numerical representation inked in the skin, reminding us everything is going to be okay.

While shooting *Twelve* I got word that the CW had officially picked up *The Beautiful Life* to series, and it was shooting in NYC. I flew back to LA to pack up my apartment and then put myself back on a plane to New York as fast as I fucking could. Everything happened so fast that I went straight from JFK to the one loft apartment that had looked incredible to me from a listing I found on Craigslist. It was in the Financial District and had sprawling East River views. I rolled up to the place with vintage Gucci luggage I had just bought. I got out of the taxi on South Street to meet the broker, then took the prewar elevator up to the apartment, looked around the raw space for about thirty seconds, and said, "I'll take it."

"Just like that?" the broker asked.

*Just. Like. That.* I signed a lease and the broker gave me the keys the next day.

*The Beautiful Life* was when I started making real money. I'm talking twenty grand an episode—more than enough to make Grandma proud. I felt like I had the keys to the entire fucking city.

Speaking of Grandma, I'd stopped over in Chicago on my way back to New York and picked out a bunch of stuff from her vintage hoard to furnish my new place. Always gotta take family with you, you know? And I was still Nico, so I quickly went to work making that raw loft a sick art space. I bought some eight-foot-tall wooden fencing from Home Depot and split the space into three large rooms—two bedrooms and a sprawling living room—and painted the apartment in bright colors and geometric patterns. This was my first real New York loft, and I was going to make it a gallery. I hung artwork all around the apartment, overlapping pieces at odd angles as if they had just fallen from an earthquake in heaven, or rather the underworld. Highly curated, highly imagined, highly free.

It was around that time that I started getting pretty fucking high. I graduated from just smoking weed and drinking alcohol to discovering cocaine. New York City has a way of luring you to its demons pretty wondrously—the bars are open till four, then there are after-hours spots, trains and cabs take you everywhere—and the only way to stay up was to stay up. Everyone was doing it, and the fantasy must continue, at all costs. We knew all the promoters at all the clubs, and there we were, getting rich, getting famous, getting close, and getting fucked up.

The second we were back at work on *The Beautiful Life*, Starlet and I started dating. She had known I was experiencing life to the fullest while shooting *Twelve*, but we weren't exclusive, so it was this "don't ask, don't tell" situation. But as soon as we reunited, there was no stopping it. She brought out the big, overgrown kid in me.

*The Beautiful Life* is a show about models, partially based on Ashton Kutcher's life. (See what I mean by life imitating art?

Or, more accurately, art imitating life? I'd been modeling in LA, after all.) The guy playing Ashton was the lead male on the show, and I was his number two. But, like I said earlier, the real star power on the show was the women. Starlet's and my characters on the show weren't supposed to be dating, but the second we began our relationship in real life, the writers started reconfiguring storylines for us to be together on the show. So what did we decide to do? Get matching tattoos that read *La Bella Vita*, which means "the beautiful life" in Italian.

We went everywhere together. And everywhere we went, people were just handing all these underage actors drugs and alcohol. This happens in the world of Hollywood—which is arguably more of a state of mind than it is an actual place—and it's not something people really talk about. Like, who's looking out for these young kids? It seemed like nobody was. And I was having too much fun to think about any of the things Jean had warned me about back in LA. We immediately started reaping the benefits of young Hollywood. Getting flown on all-expenses-paid trips down to Miami to party; the movie premieres, photo shoots, and fashion shows; gifting suites and sponsored events in the city. As long as we looked good, got our pictures taken, everything else was free. And nothing tastes better than free.

The first hiccup in my carefree life in the city came when my loft got the infamous New York City bedbugs everyone talks about, and it is as bad as they say it is. So I moved in with Starlet, who had an apartment in Chelsea. We were becoming a public couple, and I loved getting photographed on red carpets with her, fulfilling this heterosexual archetype of the square-jawed leading man and the beautiful blond actress. I was creating the very image that was expected of me, and as a result, my repressed queerness seemed to disappear, drowned out by the drugs and alcohol, clouded by the fame and fortune. And to be totally honest with y'all, it was liberating. It felt amazing. The party, like the bar I grew up in, cultivates this sense of supposed freedom, a distorted delight. However provisional it was, I felt happy.

I TURNED TWENTY-ONE while filming in New York, and was given an entire restaurant and club for the party. Although I had been partying underage for a few years, I was officially legal. I had to bring in my people—my mom, stepdad, and brother—to celebrate with me. The only person I didn't invite was Bethany. We weren't really talking at this point. They had started dating a friend of ours in LA and were living in Long Beach, starting their new life as a fitness mogul and opening studios in Orange County.

Here's a fun fact about Bethany: they were a professional cheerleader growing up. Like, full-blown *Bring It On*, Universal Cheerleaders Association, top-of-the-pyramid pixie flier. Bethany's always been a top, come to think of it. The capitalistic world of advertising and nine-to-five jobs wasn't challenging them physically or emotionally in the ways they would have liked. So they went back to their roots, and found revelation in the Pilates-inspired Megaformer, which would wind up shaping the rest of their professional life.

Back then, we were keeping in touch via email every few months. Right around my birthday, I had sent them this:

Just woke up with you running all through my head.

Thinking about you always, baby, whether you think so or not.

Just busy playing this Hollywood game.

I love you more than anything.

I think I'm coming to LA for Labor Day.

Respond, please.

Nico

Bethany responded a day later with this:

Keep playing whatever game you need to play right now, but I have to sit this one out. My life is crazy enough as is, without being left hanging.

Be good to yourself. I will always love you.

Bethany

This simple exchange speaks volume. I've always been the first one to reach out after a stretch of keeping Bethany at arm's length. Here, I extended a hand, and Bethany told me it wasn't time. And this was all mutually understood and respected, with unconditional love.

Meanwhile, my birthday party was epic. My family was staying at a hotel together for the weekend, and being able to show them my new life was pure validation; I wanted them to be proud of me and my accomplishments. At the party a lot of people were doing Ecstasy, handed out by one of the higher-ups on the show. He was this older gay guy, someone I really loved and respected, and I heard him saying that night that I was an opportunist, that I would sleep with anyone—girl or *guy*—to get ahead. "All that matters," he said, "is whether or not they're the star of the show."

I was hurt and obviously embarrassed when I heard that, and I think part of the sting was because he was gay. Was it that he saw something in me that other people didn't? Something I thought was invisible? Or was he just giving me the common flak most bisexual people have to deal with on a daily basis, based on the idea that they are in some kind of weird limbo just waiting to claim full gayness? However, I *was* taking advantage of every opportunity that came my way— jobs, parties, women, all of it—and why shouldn't I? The world was *mine*. But I wasn't ready to step into my queer identity quite yet. I had genuinely forgotten it existed at the time. I just kept burying it further and further. But anything alive underground will fight to find the sun, fight to breathe, and that's what ultimately happened for me.

Later that night, I saw an old friend of mine from back in Chicago. I grabbed him by the shoulders and mid-conversation asked, "Dude, I haven't changed, right?"

My friend looked me dead in the eyes, yelling over the dubstep in the club but careful enough not to blast me in front of anyone. "Cocaine, Nico," he said. "*That's* what's changed."

Not long after that, I was at the Boom Boom Room, this

chic lounge/club on the top of the Standard hotel in the Meat-packing District, with Ashton Kutcher and the rest of the cast. I asked Ashton what his best piece of advice for me was. "Don't ever put anything up your nose," he said. I'd literally just come out of the bathroom from doing a handful of key bumps. Ashton's a smart dude, and he very quickly realized I was high. He got in my face and started yelling at me, telling me I was flushing my entire career down my nose in front of everyone, including Demi Moore and Bruce Willis. I was embarrassed, of course, but also high off my face, so I stood up to him. Cocaine has a way of making everything razor sharp. In my mind I was hyper-calm and in control, telling him this wasn't the place to have an argument like this, when in actuality my jaw was probably doing the Macarena as I was blaming everyone else. *DENY, DENY, DENY!* I woke up the next morning so ashamed I thought maybe I would lose my job. I sent him a long email apologizing.

He sent me a short reply almost immediately, saying, *Life is not a dress rehearsal, Nico.*

It's true. Life *isn't* a dress rehearsal—it's the main event, and it happens every day, over and over again till the day we die. And anyone who has done theater for an extended period of time knows that the show always changes, that every performance has a new energy, a new lesson. We learn things every day that affect what happens tomorrow. That was the last time I ever let the party affect the work. I made sure I would never put myself in that situation again. I had way too much at stake, way too much to lose. I had worked my ass off to get that far, and I wasn't going to throw it all away that easily.

. . .

NOT LONG AFTER THAT, my entire life got taken away from me. Or at least, that's what it felt like. We were on set, and this producer steps up in the middle of everything and shouts, "That's a wrap!" The show had been canceled, just seven episodes in, because of budget issues. They didn't warn any of us. Just sent this emissary of doom to deliver the message. He walked off set just as quickly as he'd rolled up on us.

It took me about two seconds after that news came down to realize I was done with New York. Starlet was pretty much done, too. That night, back at our apartment after a long night out, we decided to cut off all her hair. A shedding of sorts. Bethany and I had both chopped off all our hair years prior, and I knew how freeing it was. (Come to think of it, I've somehow convinced a few women I've dated to cut off all their hair. Obviously there's a queer undertone to all that.) I stood behind her as she sat in a kitchen chair, draped a towel around her shoulders, then took a pair of scissors and drunkenly cut away her long blond hair in chunks that scattered as they fell to the floor. It was as if now that the show was over, we could shed the characters, become ourselves again. Or the new versions of ourselves we were creating. She had been playing this hyper-feminine character offscreen as well—the image of the perfect Hollywood starlet—but maybe that wasn't really who she was. "Fuck this hair," she said. *Fuck it.*

Of all the cast of *The Beautiful Life*, I was the first to leave the city. In only three days, I had packed up my shit and was on a plane back to LA. Starlet came not long after that, and I moved into her seventeenth-floor high-rise apartment. We had each adopted a puppy in New York and, after moving back to LA, decided to get two more. Yes, you read that right. Four fucking puppies in a condo on the seventeenth floor. So many pee pads. Our work lives had fallen apart, and we were grasping at anything and everything to make our home life more substantial. But four puppies was just fucking ridiculous. Or rather, we were fucking ridiculous.

Starlet and I continued hitting the party hard. Neither of us was working, and the party started being all we were doing. It was great at first. We were madly in love, we had created a real family, the six of us, and we had everything we wanted—the world was our oyster. Not long after we moved back to LA, I had my first experience with the paparazzi, coming out of a club late at night, high as fuck, holding her hand. It seemed like thirty guys just came out of nowhere, cameras flashing. She was used to that sort of thing, and was like, *"Whatever."* But I felt fucking *amazing*, and actually stepped *toward* them. If you look at those old photos of us, I'm literally a step ahead of her in almost all of them.

The Hollywood club scene in LA was way gayer than the one we had been part of in New York. That's not to say New York is less queer than Hollywood; in so many ways it is exponentially more the land of fruits and nuts than LA is. But there are *so* many gay people in Hollywood, running things behind the scenes, and also running the clubs. It was pretty natural for me to downplay the fact that Starlet was on my arm, and talk and flirt with these guys to get us into places and to score drugs. It was so easy, and I loved it. She saw what

I was doing, of course, but we never really talked about it. I guess it was easy for both of us to pretend it was just a means to an end. I mean, if the dudes had been straight, she would have been the one playing the beautiful person card, right?

I did try to tell her once, back when we were still living in New York, that I'd hooked up with a guy in high school, and she totally freaked out on me. Like, started screaming. Which had everything to do with her cultural programming, so I don't blame her for it. But that was definitely one of the reasons I buried my queerness deeper and deeper until it went totally underground. I took back the bisexual revelation quickly, made a joke out of it and said it hadn't happened, that I'd just wanted to see how she'd react. "What the fuck, Nico?" she said. We never talked about it again. But I thought maybe there was a way I could play with my gender in a not so threatening way. It wasn't long after that that I got in full drag for the first time.

It was Los Angeles Pride (it's a march, not a parade), and because of all the new friends we had gathered in Hollywood, I wanted to celebrate it flamboyantly. I remember putting on Starlet's clothes and makeup and feeling so fucking free. I was an actor, playing dress-up was natural. It reminded me of being a little kid and playing dress-up with my mom and brother. But this time I was old enough that it meant something different, immediately implying that I wanted a dick in my ass. Starlet was okay with it at first, but it was clear it started to chip away at her impression of who I was. What she wanted. What was societally acceptable. What we were taught was right and wrong. What was expected of us as this straight Hollywood couple. What it meant for a leading man in the making.

I kept looking for a job, auditioning all the time, but for the first time since I'd come to Hollywood, the work had dried up. Fortune is fickle, you know. Things started to get pretty dark for both of us. I was drinking way too much, doing a lot of coke, and getting over the hangovers by eating anything and everything I could to soak up the filth. From the second the real partying started, my connection to the natural world, my devotion to a raw food diet, slowly disappeared as well. It was like all these parts of me that had defined my existence were being eaten by Hollywood, which asked for your soul in exchange for recognition. I was gaining weight, literally and metaphorically. I hadn't started drinking during the day, all day, quite yet, but that would come soon enough. The only connection I really had to the industry at that point *was* the party.

THAT FALL, my aunt and uncle—the self-proclaimed smartest man in the world and the Goddess woman who'd written Bethany a letter welcoming them to the family—the two people I loved so much that I literally couldn't imagine my life without them, packed up and left Chicago without saying a word to the rest of the family. Just cut themselves off and moved to Florida. No explanation. Even now, I can't tell you why they left. Everyone in the family has theories, each of them kind of bizarre and conflicting. But no one really knows, because they've still never told us flat out.

I was totally wrecked. Soon after they moved, my uncle was planting a palm tree on the property they'd bought, and there was an accident. The giant tree fell on his legs and crushed them both. Even though they'd left us, I called them immediately and offered to come down and help them in whatever way I could. But my uncle didn't want me to see him like that. The gorilla warrior judo champion, disabled, beyond weak. My first instinct had been to help the man who had watered me from the time I was a small seed. My second instinct was deeper, more primal, from my gut: *Karma is a motherfucker.* My aunt and uncle had taught me that, too.

No one in my family was in the greatest of states when I decided to bring Starlet home with me for Christmas. It was the first holiday ever without my aunt and uncle, and I was determined to continue the family tradition of poker. I showed up already drunk with hundreds of singles to hand out. I was determined to keep our family together like nothing had ever happened. It was a disaster, of course. To further complicate things, my family didn't like Starlet—which didn't really have anything to do with who she was, but more with the person I had become and her role in the changes they saw in me.

It was the classic story of the kid starting to get famous and being an asshole. I had seen so much, so fast, that I was a self-righteous motherfucker. I had gotten the taste of life on the other side of the tracks and couldn't understand why everyone wouldn't want it. But I was also still me, the Nico I'd always been, the one who'd Freed Will with their distant father, the one who had the divine plant spirits tattooed on their back, the one who wanted to be pushed forward, into the future.

Starlet and I were at home in her high-rise one night, our

four little puppies running around the party chaos of our apartment. I was high and drinking, but I could still feel it, my inner self pushing back at me, desperately reaching for some sort of exposure. We were really close. Best friends. But it's hard to decipher exactly what was love and what was substance—whether it was the party that kept us close or the celebrity image or the unconditional childlike enthusiasm. I fucking loved that girl. But I wasn't loving myself. And it's almost impossible to take care of anyone else or a relationship without a certain level of self-care and respect. Something I would come to realize very intensely in the years to follow.

"Baby," I said, "I'm losing my magic."

"Nico, don't try to blame that on me."

"I'm not," I said. "I'm not blaming you."

But I was blaming Starlet for some of it. Not her specifically, but what she represented. The scene, the celebrity. What was expected of both of us as these archetypes. She had to be feminine, I had to be masculine. We both had to conform to what was expected of us. The leading man and the leading lady. The money and the lifestyle and the drugs and the alcohol. And none of that was in line with how I was raised. How I blossomed. My spiritual connection was disappearing. I'd started forgetting the shit that was most important. I was just consuming instead of creating. I'd been seduced maybe from the first moment I saw that Gucci luggage. Seduced by capitalism, by young, white, privileged-as-fuck Hollywood, by the binary. By image. If you look at photos of me from that time, I look straight as an arrow, all my feyness pushed down deep. The perfect heterosexual picture.

Trust me, karma *is* a motherfucker.

Right around this time, I booked my first leading role in a huge studio franchise film, *Scream 4*. Everyone and their cousin auditioned for that movie, and after six or seven auditions and meetings with producers, the role was mine. I had never seen any of the *Scream* movies before I booked the job. The audition scenes were from the first movie and I literally had no idea. Apparently whatever I did worked, though. This was a Wes Craven film, featuring Neve Campbell, Courteney Cox, David Arquette, and a huge list of other celebrities joining the franchise—a huge milestone in my career.

There was definitely another Starlet in that movie, and we may not have been in a full relationship, but we got close. We were young and partying way too hard. This was also right around the time David and Courteney were getting a divorce, and let's just say we were all fucking loose. It was like college for the older generation; they had been down this road three times before and welcomed us into the fraternity, parties and all. Those were some of the loudest couple of months of my life. When that movie wrapped, I all of a sudden had a brand-new group of friends in LA, a new house in Calabasas, and newfound celebrity status. Which meant more of everything.

One of my dreams at that time was to do a shoot with *Inked* magazine. I had started to take the art of tattooing really seriously and was getting quite a collection of ink. A portrait of my grandpa on my arm by Kat Von D. Antlers on my feet to protect the ground I was walking on. A Darwinian dove skull to commemorate my last name, which means "turtle dove" in Italian. A cross of typewriter keys on my calf that read *love good people* (the only drunk tattoo I ever got). My publicity team had an in at *Inked* and hooked me up. I was elated. I ended up becoming tight with the stylist on the shoot, this amazing woman, Frankie. She was older, had been in the scene for a minute, and just happened to be a raging alcoholic. I fucking loved her. She'd come over to my house, and we'd lie around on the couch, drinking our faces off, talking fashion and art, and bitching and complaining about everything. Looking back, she was like every gay dude's best girlfriend, the one you can be more yourself with than your own partner. Starlet couldn't stand her. But Frankie was a fixture at my place, sometimes crashing out for the night and then starting the morning with a Bloody Mary or a few beers. It seemed like a good idea to me. But the thing about getting drunk in the morning is that by the afternoon, you're too wasted to do anything but keep on drinking.

Frankie wasn't necessarily queer, but a lot of her people were. Hanging with her allowed the part of myself that had been hidden for so long to slowly creep back into the picture. Soon after I met her, she introduced me to this older gay photographer. He was hella famous, and I desperately wanted him to shoot me. I went to his house in the hills one night, and he and I started partying while we were shooting. The session was hours and hours long, and after a certain point, I started to break a little inside. Being with this older gay man with alcohol lubricant, my defenses started to drop. I'd been playing at being straight for what felt like forever, and I just wanted to talk to this man, who could maybe tell me something about what I was going through. Through tears, it just kind of fell out of my mouth: "I think maybe I'm gay. And I don't know what to do about it. My family, my career . . ."

As I talked, he put down his camera and walked over to me. I hadn't been thinking about sleeping with him. I mean, I was attracted to him, but that's not what this was about. But he put his hand on my face and asked if he could kiss me. Before he could even finish the question, I slammed my face against his. And as his stubbled chin caressed mine, it all started to make sense. *I* started to make sense again.

I woke up the next morning in a panic. I'd passed out in his bed, and my phone had died at some point. I had a ton of missed calls from Starlet. Shit. The photographer and I wound up shooting again that morning, and still to this day when I go back and look at the progression of pictures, entire lives were lived in that twenty-four hours. A beginning, a middle, and an end. Afterward, I jumped in my car and drove to her apartment as fast as I could. Starlet was mad pissed—I told her I'd gotten drunk and crashed at the photographer's, but she didn't quite believe nothing had happened. We were strictly monogamous, and neither of us had ever spent the night away without letting the other know. The thing was, she thought I'd spent the night with Frankie. So, a few days later, when Frankie was over and we were hanging on the couch, drunk as fuck, lounging on top of each other in hysterics, Starlet walked in and saw us, and she just snapped.

"If this is who you are, Nico, then I'm fucking done. Fucking done with this."

And that was the last time I ever saw her. I could go on and on about how many times I tried to apologize over the years.

About how many times I wished I could pick up the phone and say, "Hi, babe, how are you, what's new?" She remains one of my only exes with whom I don't have any sort of relationship. Like, one day she was my everything, and the next she was gone. She needed the clean break, and I can understand that, but I also lost my best friend. She still shows up in my dreams on the regular, and from the bottom of my heart I wouldn't trade the time we had together for anything.

I spent so many years repressing my sexuality early on in my career. I felt that in order to become famous I had to play the straight male in my personal life, too. The industry was a lot different back then (pre-social media), and there was even more pressure on heteronormativity than there is today. There are undoubtedly many celebrities who are still unsure how to manage being queer in an industry that doesn't value it, never mind being bisexual. Biphobia is very real. Starlet caught a whiff of it on me and was completely turned off. For years, I internalized that bias, as if my desire for men would disqualify my desire for women. But I have always been bisexual. It just took a long time to get over my own internalized biphobia, and to be honest, I'm still working through it.

But let's back up a minute, to the morning after I slept with the photographer. I was a mess, and it wasn't because I was afraid of what was going to happen with my relationship. The writing had been on the wall between Starlet and me for some time. I really did think some of my magic had left because of her, and part of that was because I knew I could never really be myself with her. I guess I had known that since the minute she freaked out about me maybe being bisexual. Or maybe when she got more and more uncomfortable seeing me in that dress at Pride. Jamie had loved that gender-exploring side of me, remember, and so had Bethany. They were able to accept and love everything about me that I could accept and love about myself.

Bethany and I hadn't really spoken in over a year. Maybe once or twice, here and there. They'd moved to Dallas at some point after I'd left LA, because things had started to get dark for them, too. The dude they wound up dating, our mutual friend, was an intense drug addict and possibly even a Satanist. Their relationship got super violent and abusive, and Bethany needed to get away. At that point Bethany had also not been taking care of themselves. An eating disorder had resurfaced, and the intersection between that and getting out of the relationship was very clear. They got an opportunity to help open a Megaformer studio in Dallas, and it was a no-brainer for them to accept. The only reason I knew any of this was because I'd call Bethany sometimes when I was just high enough, and we'd catch up a little, talking about my life and lovers, and what was up with Bethany and their life and relationships. But Bethany thought I'd become a full-tilt asshole, this Hollywood guy, and had mostly sworn off me around the time of my twenty-first birthday party.

Still, though, Bethany and I had this SOS rule: if one of us called twice in a row, it meant the other had to pick up. I had to call Bethany three times the morning after I hooked up with the photographer before they picked up. Thank God. I was cracked open, felt like I was falling apart, and I needed to talk to someone in my family. Bethany was the only person in the world I felt like I could trust. And it all just came pouring out. I told them about the photographer, about other men, about my first gay experience in high school, about being afraid I was gay or bisexual and definitely not knowing what to do with it.

And Bethany caught me, caught me right when I was falling. Caught me as they have continued to do for the last twelve years in one way or another. Just as I felt I was going to hit the ground, there they were with open arms. They knew I was at a breaking point, and they showed up for me. Bethany's nurturing instinct has a way of kicking in at times of panic, especially if I'm the one in distress. They have the ability to see past what is wrong and take care of the person rather than the situation. There wasn't an ounce of disgust or shame or question from Bethany regarding my sexuality. They just listened, and assured me that they would be there for me. No matter what.

A few weeks later, after Starlet and I broke up, Bethany called me. I didn't answer the first call, but as soon as it rang again, I knew it was important. Karma really is a motherfucker. I picked up the phone and all I could hear were soft tears.

"Baby, I'm pregnant."

Everything that happened next is sort of a blur. I booked a ticket to Dallas immediately and was there the next day. The baby wasn't mine, obviously, but it didn't matter. After deep consideration, Bethany knew they couldn't keep the baby. I went to the doctor's office with them the day I landed. I had dealt with a partner's abortion firsthand a number of years before and was all too familiar with the process. It's a painful one, emotionally, physically, and spiritually. And knowing Bethany's history with the church, I knew there was going to be another layer to the baggage. They opted for an at-home medical abortion, the same procedure I had seen the first time. I knew it hurt, and I knew it was a deeply emotional process.

The next day, we stayed in their downtown Dallas apartment and waited. The experience varies from person to person. Unfortunately, it was physically and emotionally very painful for Bethany. I set up candles and played music and chanted prayers as the time passed to honor the life lost. And more important, in that moment, to honor the life gained.

As traumatic an experience as it was, Bethany has never regretted the decision. This was their body, their life, their choice. Timing is everything when bringing children into this world, and when Bethany and I are ready, our children will come to us at the perfect moment.

This was a massive turning point in our relationship, and in our lives. It had been years since we were this intimate, though it felt as if not a day had passed. That we had been doing this seemingly for lifetimes. It solidified our forever quality—that no matter what had happened in our separate individual lives, no matter what had transpired in the time lost, no matter how much we did or didn't talk, we showed up. We honored. We celebrated. We were family, forever.

## CHAPTER 4

I DECIDED TO RENT THE HOUSE IN CALABASAS AS A WAY TO GET OUT OF Hollywood. It was forty-five minutes away from the boulevard, which was both just close enough and adequately far away. That house was my first real taste of a home with land. I had an acre on a mountain with epic, stunning views of the valley and a pond in the backyard that I stocked with goldfish and turtles. I had a whole slew of pets come in and out of that house. I bought a 150-pound tortoise at one point, but the dogs hated me for it, so I exchanged him for an albino boa constrictor I named Hadrian. Jean had taught me all about Antinous, the young boy whom the Roman emperor Hadrian took as a lover, and who was later found drowned in a river. No one actually knows if it was suicide or murder, but queers since Oscar Wilde have been writing about Antinous as this tragic figure of homo love. After Antinous died, Hadrian had him deified as the incarnation of Osiris, Egyptian God of the Underworld. I was actually very afraid of snakes, but I made myself buy one to get over the fear. It seemed fitting to name him Hadrian at the time. And it would seem even more fitting a few years later, when I traveled through the underworld myself.

The house had been built in the eighties, properly outfitted with a bar in the living room, two fireplaces, and enough bedrooms to start a family. I'd been living there for a few months before I got a call from my mom. Now, some would say the amount I communicate with my mother on a daily basis is unhealthy. But I wouldn't have it any other way. My mom is hands down the funniest person I've ever met in my life—her comic timing is impeccable—and on good days, we laugh and laugh. We know everything about each other. We'll discuss health and spirituality, and when she's having a hard day, I'll guide her through a meditation with the crystals I've bought her over the years. She complains, I complain, we make each other feel better. We show up, unconditionally, sometimes to our detriment.

So, she called me and told me she was moving to LA with my stepdad, brother, and their two huge mastiffs. And I had this big house, so why not move in with me until they found a new place? It's not as if she asked me or I offered—it was just expected. That's what family does. Sounds like a great idea, right?

My stepdad had retired from working on the floor of the stock exchange in Chicago and wanted to relax. His work hours had been ungodly. He would wake up at four a.m. in order to sit in traffic and head to a job he hated. Lots of screaming and toxic masculine energy all day, every day. But he was one of the good guys.

My parents rolled up to the house in an RV they had rented for the cross-country trip. I had my two small dogs, they had their four-pawed dinosaurs, and I was nervous about how everyone would get along. When the door of the motorhome opened and one of the big mastiffs rushed straight for the Chihuahua, almost killing her, I knew the next few months would be difficult. But before I had time to freak out, I booked a new job.

A few weeks after my family moved in, I flew to New Mexico to shoot this supernatural thriller called *Odd Thomas*. There was another boy working on the film whom I immediately bonded with. Red was this bright-eyed, towheaded mush of love and excitement. This was his first real job in the industry, and I took him under my wing. Red and I got super close; I felt like I could talk to him about almost everything. People on the set started joking about us always being together. Our first week on set, we both started sleeping with women who were working on the movie, as if to prove that we didn't want to sleep with each other.

Red kind of reminded me of myself. He was goofy and ridiculously funny, and behind his masculine demeanor was this super-feminine side, especially when he was drunk. And we were always drinking after work. You get really close with people working on sets—it's like a traveling carnival, this super-intense experience where all the carnies get to know one another really fast, maybe in part because you know it'll be over soon. Love with an expiration date. It's safe to say Red and I would have never hooked up if it hadn't been for the booze. Still, it didn't happen until the last week of the two months we spent working on the film, and we'd both taken some Molly. We were already so close that hooking up felt like a natural extension of our intimacy.

But I woke up the next morning worried and disarmed by the hangover. Red and I still had to shoot the following day. I knew he'd never been with a man before, and I was worried that maybe he'd freak out, have some kind of emotional backlash. This was a guy who'd made a point to tell me he most definitely wasn't gay, after all. But he surprised me. He was so comfortable during work that day, more open with me than he'd ever been before. It was almost like this weight had been lifted off him. And that made me feel more comfortable, which brought us closer together.

We were in our carnival bubble, outside of real life and real time. After the film wrapped, we stayed in New Mexico for two more weeks, driving around the desert and having a lush love affair. I'd never slept in the same bed with a man for nights and nights in a row, and full disclosure, it made me think of my dad. There's something about laying my head on a man's hairy chest that will always put me back in my dad's bedroom, the one that smelled of tanning bed coconut oil and tobacco, right before the divorce. At that point, I hadn't seen or spoken to Pops in years, and I tried not to think about him too often. Lying beside Red, I felt a peace and safety that I hadn't felt in a long time. We even FaceTimed the women we'd been sleeping with while shooting, tangled up in bed together, and said, "Look what happened, y'all." They were both properly confused, but surprisingly supportive. It was beautiful—there was no shame or guilt . . . yet.

Red and I went back to LA together, already in love. This was something brand-new for both of us, and the excitement majorly raised the stakes. The lease for his apartment on the west side was up, so I helped him pack up his shit. The first night we were there, Red took me into his bedroom, and I told him I wanted to bottom for him. I'd never done that before, and I was scared, but I also wanted to be vulnerable with him— something in me needed this. I'd never had anyone *inside* me before, and when I let Red do this, I felt like I understood something I hadn't known before. The kind of trust it takes, the openness it takes to bring someone else inside of you. It was a breaking-open for me, a kind of sacred stillness that came in after it was over. I was aware of the vulnerability of my own body.

You know how it's acceptable, or more acceptable, for men to have sex with other men as long as they maintain the position of dominance—of only topping, never being entered—how men who bottom are looked down upon? I think part of the reason for this is that the act does upend what it means to be a "man." To bottom, you have to admit your vulnerability, to welcome it, to give up control, and it changed me, made me feel another part of myself.

We are taught in sexual education that men have a penis, to insert. The penis is masculine; the one who holds the stick holds the power. But what we're not taught is the sacred power of our prostate. So let's talk about the prostate, y'all. This walnut-size gland is located inside the rectum and secretes the seminal fluid that nourishes and protects sperm. Prostate massage and stimulation can be both exciting and beneficial to one's health. Although it's widely considered our own internal G-spot, the only way we learn about this erotic zone is to explore it alone or with a partner.

In the heteronormative world, anything remotely having to do with a man's asshole is considered gay. I'm not sure how we got to that point, but it probably has to do with religious beliefs, societal standards, and the idea that enjoyment associated with an "unclean" place has made this taboo. People associate anal pleasure with vulnerability and loss of power. Only by quite literally delving into the depths of my own body have I come to discover its power. Some of the greatest orgasms I've ever had have been through prostate stimulation. It was only after I bottomed for the first time that the intersection of anal sex and gender became clear. It didn't take me out of my own masculinity, but instead showed me that even in my masculine body, I could discover the extent of my own femininity from a place of release and vulnerability. My masculinity can be feminine, my femininity can be masculine. A lesson straight people, especially men, could really benefit from.

The next day, we drove to my house, Red at the wheel. It was early morning, and we were both sober, and he reached across and took my hand. I'd never held a man's hand like that, not in my entire life, and I felt overcome, feeling his palm against mine, looking down and seeing those two hands—masculine hands—holding each other. Although we're taught that men aren't supposed to be tender with each other, I felt no shame, just peacefulness and gratitude. There was country music playing on the radio, and we looked right into each other's eyes. *This is who we are.* I'd never been able to look into the eyes of a man I'd slept with like that before. *This is who I am.*

My mom and stepdad had just moved out of my place in Calabasas (thank you, Jesus) to a big property about forty-five minutes away, so I asked Red to move in with me. Rocco was still living at my place, so he knew about me and Red, but it was a big secret that I kept from the rest of our family. Rocco had always known I was different; we both are, in our own ways. Red most definitely was not out to his family, either, and we set up an extra bedroom to look like it was his for when our families came to visit. Red and I didn't even talk about the fact that we were doing this; it was just understood that this was the way it had to be. We had to pretend for them, and for everyone else. I wonder, though, who were we actually protecting? Our families, or ourselves? Now that we were back in our "real" lives, off the set, being a couple carried an intense amount of stress for both of us. A stress that neither one of us really knew how to talk about or deal with. So we didn't.

My mom adored Red at first, and we spent a lot of time at her new place, sometimes days and days. I'm not sure what was up with my mom then—maybe she was missing her bar back in Chicago—but she and my stepdad were having parties at their place all the time. One party just bled into another. I suppose my brother and I were the ones really bringing the party, but our parents were supporting it, and we were all getting fucked up together. When I would go back to Chicago to visit the rest of my family for an energetic reset, one of my older cousins would grill me about my newfound celebrity: "Who the fuck are you? Is this what Hollywood does to you? Makes you a

drunk douchebag? What the fuck is happening? What happened to Nico?" Because my immediate family was in California partying with me, they didn't see how bad it really was yet.
So when my cousin showed up for me, I couldn't hear it. People were worried about me, and at times I was worried about
me. But I kept drinking, numbing and numbing and numbing.

My mom and stepdad wound up growing weed on their
property—legally, mind you (this is California)—and a lot of it.
I started getting high with my mom and stepdad, which was
honestly fucking amazing, and there was a good amount of
alcohol flowing. Red and I were there all the time, pretending
that we weren't a couple, just really close "best friends." The
pressure started to build with the lying we felt we had to do.
We were in love, and we slept in the same bed, but we couldn't
tell our families we'd found each other. We were afraid they
wouldn't love *us* anymore if they found out. We were afraid
what it would do to our careers.

Keeping this secret, and not being able to talk about it,
started tearing us apart. After a while, Red and I could only
fuck when we were blackout drunk, and I would wake up in the
morning feeling bad and guilty about all of it. We had started
out open, honest, tender, and loving, but as time went on, we
went deeper and deeper into the closet all over again. Repressing who we were maybe even more than ever before, because
now this wasn't just a fantasy. It was very real.

I remember the first time I found out that being gay was
even a thing. I was eight years old, riding with my mom in her

candy-apple-red GMC Jimmy, and I saw two guys on the street holding hands. I asked my mom something like, "Why would two guys ever be together? They can't make babies." I was just a little kid and had zero understanding of sex. I once found my mom's diaphragm in the car door and she told me it was a valve for the air conditioner.

Anyway, my mom kind of freaked out. She went off on how disgusting being gay was. She said the two guys walking up the street were downright revolting. "Have babies?!" she said. "Even holding hands is disgusting!" They looked normal enough to me, but my *mom* saying they were gross, that stuck. And then there was all the stuff my stepdad and grandma were always saying, and the kids at school who called me a faggot after I stopped playing hockey and started doing theater. I couldn't tell my mom about Red because if she thought I was *filthy*, then how could she possibly love me?

I think it's entirely possible my mom always sort of knew something was up with me. I mean, I was a theater kid, I was always flamboyant, and—let's be honest—she probably noticed how I went after my stepdad's *International Male* catalogs when they showed up in the mail. I was only twelve when she bought me my first *Playboy*. We were at the Family Pantry, our local corner store, and I'd picked it up off the magazine rack as a joke. It was the December Christmas gala issue with Carmen Electra on the cover wearing nothing but glitter pumps and vamping inside a giant clear ornament. Mom saw the nudie mag in my hand and asked if I wanted it. I said yes, and she bought it for me. Pretty progressive of her, if you ask me—

further proof that she is cool as shit. Also proof that she wanted me to be into women and women only.

That programming from my family and culture ran deep, as it had for Red. We both hated ourselves for having to hide being gay, and I think that might have caused us to start hating each other. We started taking shit out on each other. I was in between jobs, drinking and doing drugs all the time. And doing this with my family, who I loved so much and also felt hurt by in ways that I couldn't really face.

Things came to a head about six months into living with Red, at a holiday party at my mom and stepdad's house. The Christmas tree was decorated with all our childhood ornaments, lights in greens and reds were strung all around the house, and the bar was fully stocked. We invited about thirty people—friends from the neighborhood, Hollywood, and some family flew in for the party. I showed up already buzzed in this vintage white rabbit fur and red cashmere Santa costume. We went swimming and played a big game of kickball, as one does when the desert weather is 75 degrees on Christmas, and I continued to get more and more fucked up. Falling deeper and deeper in the closet of shame and guilt.

Things between Red and me were bad. I blame myself, and that night I did something I still feel ashamed of. I don't quite remember how it happened, but I slept with one of my stepdad's coworkers from Chicago. Of all the sexual experiences I've had, this is the only one that makes me feel uncomfortable. She was older than me, and I was blacked out. Later, I was sure I was an asshole, but I couldn't actually remember what had happened. What I *did* know was that I'd slept with her at the party to make sure my family knew I was sleeping with women. It wasn't a secret when she and I went off together. Red knew about it, too. Later that night, he and I got into a terrible fight, right in front of my mom. Red left, and then my stepdad was yelling at me—it was like I was at war with everyone I loved. And I was too fucked up to know what was going on. It was at that moment that my mom started to resent Red—hate him, even.

The entire time I've known my stepdad, we've only had three fights. The holiday party was number two. He is very much a realist, leaning on the side of pessimism. He had a strict upbringing in the Catholic Church, and I think some of that always stayed with him. He also has an obsessive-compulsive personality: he's the kind of guy who picks up one hobby and then doesn't do anything else until the next one comes along. If my stepdad is doing something he loves and he's doing it well, he's the happiest man on the planet. If he fucks up, watch out, world. I think it's totally possible that living in a party house in LA was slowly driving him crazy. It just wasn't his style—that was all my mom, my brother, and me, but he was going along with it.

Later that night, when the party had died down some, my stepdad came to find me. He was furious. Up in my face, screaming. It was the only time in my life I thought we might start throwing punches. I wouldn't have even remembered what he said that night, except that the next day, he sent me an email. (He loves an email.) He could see how bad things were getting and knew it was time to intervene. Here are some of the things he said:

You show up at your parents' house at 2:00 in the afternoon, for what was supposed to be a holiday celebration. A nice, relaxing, friends and family day. Everyone here is completely sober and ready to hit the pool for some sun and a couple drinks. Not you. You are COMPLETELY SHITFACED . . . AGAIN. Not just a couple social drinks, but still reeling from a multiple-night binge to the point where you are uncoordinated. And it's not just a happy buzz. It's a "let's annoy the crap out of everybody" buzz. And good, you brought a couple friends to witness your behavior.

Start by getting the large, aggressive dogs worked into a dog fight, even though your mother has warned you a hundred times that you are going to get bitten. When it happens the animal will be a big asshole, right?

Go to the bathroom and pee all over the whole floor.

Pee into the planter at the back door that your mother works to get out and water every single day this summer.

Move on to your mother and say the most hurtful, untrue garbage that you can imagine to the point where she is devastated and truly damaged.

Do absolutely nothing to help prepare, cook, clean, or participate in any kind of meaningful way. Oh yeah, did I mention you brought along a couple friends to be embarrassed for you?

Fall over on the pool steps, busting the plastic rail on the pool your mom and Rocco worked so hard to get perfect. Pass out on our bed and refuse to move into your own room to just take a nap, and then bust down the gate when people try to help you. The gate I then quietly fixed. Alone.

Throw the lawn furniture all over the yard and break a metal chair that was part of a matching set of patio furniture, and drop cigarette butts all over the patio.

Kick a drink over on the floor of the theater and ignore your mother when she points it out to you. While I'm on my hands and knees with paper towels cleaning up your latest mess, I hear your mother in the kitchen telling you not to drink vodka straight out of the bottle. Cool.

Then when we finally get you into your personal taxi ride back home, I find the gate I fixed once, left in a pile of pieces on the floor for a second time, now beyond repair. That was it. I lost it. I can only endure so much garbage in the home I have worked so hard to provide.

Within twenty-four hours of sending this email, my stepdad showed up on my doorstep. I had called my mom immediately after receiving the email and crumbled. This was obviously some sort of desperate cry for help, but I was fucking pissed. Why wasn't *she* blasting me? Was she too caught up in her own addictions that she couldn't see how badly I needed help? And was he coming to make it better or make it worse?

We sat for a couple of hours and talked it all out. I was hurt, he was hurt, and we both desperately needed to heal. When this man's eyes welled with tears, I could see the boy in him. The softer, more human side that his hard shell hides. The boy who was told not to cry. When I cry, I wail. The elixir of both our tears meeting in that moment cleansed the situation. We talked about addiction and the path I was on. He told me stories from his past, things I would have never imagined. And together we reconciled, for the time being. We basked in our trauma and grief. A boy broken, and his dad putting the pieces back together.

This was the most father-son interaction I have ever had in my life. It ended with hugs, tears, and *I love you*s. This man was there every single step of the way. Every hockey practice and game to help me put on my skates, every theater production, every major moment in my life, he was there. For the good times and the terrible. Sometimes for the soft love (he chokes up when reading holiday cards in the cutest way I've ever seen), and sometimes for the tough love that I clearly needed. He saved our family. Today at thirty, about the same age my step-dad was when he met my mom and us, I imagine what it would look like to meet someone who has two kids and give up everything for them. I wonder if I would have the mental clarity and stamina to step up to the plate the way my stepdad did. The way that he does. Without this man—without his work ethic and drive to make a better life for all of us, without his support emotionally and fiscally, without his love for all things, I would never be where I am today. I wouldn't know what it means to fight for what I believe. I wouldn't be sober, and I might not even be alive.

At the end of the day, I'm so glad he wrote me that email; no matter how much I hated reading it, I'm glad he showed up. It changed a lot for me.

Red moved out of my house the day after our argument. He couldn't bear the way we'd been living anymore, and I was barely holding on to anything, let alone our relationship. My parents moved to LA at the same time I was growing into my queerness, and I revolted. Self-sabotaged, self-destructed. I destroyed every relationship I had, and was slowly killing myself. If I hadn't been taught by the world to hate this part of my identity and expression, would I have tried to kill it? Would I ever have allowed the spirits to take over? I'm not blaming anyone but myself, but imagine for a second what this world would look like if we didn't teach our children to hate themselves.

The entire time Red and I were living together, I was flying to Dallas every so often to see Bethany. They knew I was dating Red, but he had no idea I was sleeping with Bethany. It was an amateur, half-assed, drunken version of an open relationship, and I was being shitty to Red. He always had more of an issue with my visits to Dallas than he would let on, but I was unable to adequately explain to him, or even to myself, what was happening. One of my biggest regrets to this day is the way I treated him over the years.

Bethany knew I was in a lot of pain then, and they were in pain, too. We held each other up. They understood how toxic an environment LA had become for me and were more than happy to provide a safe refuge in Dallas. Bethany was also seeing other people; it's been that way pretty much the entire twelve years we've been in each other's lives. It was in Dallas that Bethany and I got our first of many tattoos together. Living in LA, I started calling Bethany "mustard butt." We would go on these epic hikes and wild mustard flowers are everywhere in Southern California. On one insane uphill hike somewhere up north, the only thing that kept Bethany on the mountain and not falling backward was holding on to the mustard flowers for leverage. We would pick them all day and just eat them straight from the ground. I have a deep love for bees, always have. Without them, we wouldn't be here. So we got tattoos that told a story. Bethany got a mustard flower about a foot long on their hip, from their mid back to the top of their ass. And I got a bee in flight. When we stand next to each other, it looks as if my bee is pollinating their flower.

One of the interesting things about our relationship is that Bethany had become this validation in my life that I wasn't exclusively gay. And believe me when I say that being exclusively gay wouldn't be a bad thing at all. Honestly, sometimes I think it would be so much easier. Life would be way less complex if I was one way or the other. Bisexuality can be a fucking mess internally. We're taught that we have to be one way or the other, and that anything in between isn't real. It's like this netherworld where you have one foot in the closet and one foot out, and people on each side keep pushing and pulling in both directions. What happens when a bisexual person is in a committed relationship? Does that other part of their identity disappear just because they have chosen one or the other?

Full disclosure: I usually gauge how I'm feeling about my sexual attraction by the porn I'm watching. And it can switch, mid-session, even, with no real explanation. The more work Bethany and I do to understand gender outside the binary—the space between—the easier navigating my own desire and its fluidity seems to be. But it's not perfect, and I imagine it never will be.

NOT LONG AFTER Red moved out, I got rid of the house in Calabasas and bought a 1967 Dodge Travco—that's an RV, y'all—and moved it onto my parents' property. They had a lot of land, and I spent weeks building an eight-foot-tall fence, walling myself within an acre of land. I wound up painting the fence white as a stark contrast to the reds and desert browns of the landscape. It's like I needed to still be close to my family, but also needed distance from them. Within that wall, I could be by myself, but not alone. Also, I had to protect the puppies from my parents' carnivorous mastiffs.

Red and I mended things after our big fight, and he would come stay with me sometimes. Things between us started feeling good again. But I knew I wouldn't be staying long. I hadn't worked in six or seven months, which meant a job would probably be coming in soon, and I would go wherever it took me.

I was sent the script for *The Following*, a brand-new Kevin Williamson drama starring Kevin Bacon, while I was living in the RV. I went in for my first audition and got a callback to test for the part of a bisexual serial killer. Within a week, the offer came in. This was big time. I flew to Atlanta to shoot the pilot almost immediately. FOX picked it up, and filming was scheduled to start in New York in July. I sold the RV on eBay, destroyed the wall literally and figuratively, packed up my car with the essentials and my puppies, and drove cross-country by myself. Back to the city. But this time was different. I had seen more, known more, given more, taken more. And this time, I wanted to take something else with me: Bethany.

Bethany had always wanted to live in New York. They had never visited me while I was living there, and this was the perfect opportunity to make up for lost time. I had visited Bethany in Dallas probably a dozen times by this point, and our familial bond was getting stronger. They were tired of Texas and the energy that comes with the territory; they were ready for a change. A Megaformer studio in New York had already expressed interest in Bethany, and everything seemed to be falling into place. I had no idea how long the show would last or how long I would be staying, but I said to them: "I have an apartment in Brooklyn. Come move in with me, get your life situated in New York, and we will see where it goes from there."

But I had one condition: "I have to be allowed to keep exploring relationships with men. This has to be an open relationship." Bethany was in. They appreciated my newfound comfort regarding my sexuality. Later, I would find out that my ability to expand as an individual through my sexual relations with all genders had inspired them to open a piece of themselves that had always been there, but dormant. So I moved with Bethany and the dogs to Brooklyn—one apartment, an open relationship, New York City. What's the worst that could happen?

The apartment in Brooklyn was dope. We had this huge second-story terrace, perfect for the dogs, and a fire pit. We had these amazing Israeli neighbors who quickly became like family, and all seemed to be going really well. Shooting *The Following* was my biggest challenge as an actor thus far. Being on a show like that, constantly creating and re-creating fear-based situations and toying with the energies of murder, rape, and suicide, takes a real toll on the spirit. To get through all the baggage I was bringing home from that job, I reverted to disappearing, numbing the pain with spirits. Sex, drugs, and alcohol.

I kept up the party, despite what had happened in LA, and Bethany was right there with me. At some point, Bethany and I started throwing erotic soirees at our apartment. There was lots of booze and drugs, and lots of sex, but we were having these parties with the same four or five people who we trusted. The Atomic Love Bomb was what we called ourselves, which was actually the inspiration for the *Love Bomb* podcast. Bethany and I hadn't had any kind of group sex since that time in Mexico, so it was kind of a big decision for us to start doing this. Especially since I had become more open about my sexuality.

It was right around that time that my mannerisms began to change. I've always had rather strong, excitable hands—"fancy fingers," my mom calls them. Like my energy is just shooting out of my paws at all times. I mean, most Italians communicate with exaggerated hand gestures, but this is different. I started to attribute a deeper meaning to it. I began to analyze how my voice, my inflection, and my posture and the ways in which I held myself or crossed my legs communicated who I was. The world in which we live classifies all these idiosyncrasies into the binaries of masculinity and femininity. Was there a way I could send out both—or rather, all—these energies at the same time? Every single choice we make on how we present ourselves sends signals and energies out to the world around us, and I was finally more comfortable letting the girls out, so to speak.

And the sex parties felt right, too. It was like, by doing this together, we were putting our ideas of how we wanted to be together into practice. No ownership, understanding our jealousy, queering things up. It was the first time I had ever seen Bethany with a woman, and the first time Bethany had seen me with a man. We had been exposing our masculine and feminine energies and the space between in ways that were brand-new and in tandem. The queer twin flame was rising.

I started pretty seriously dating another guy for a few months right around Hurricane Sandy. And the first night I spent at his place, my mom called. Like most moms, she's always had this kind of crazy ESP about me and Rocco. I answered, because I always answer when she calls. Her voice was weird, super controlled. Something I had never heard before.

"Nico," she said, "do you have something to tell me?"

"Um . . . about what?"

"Well, Rocco just told me some things. Things about you and Red."

"I don't know what you're talking about, Mom."

"Are you fucking gay, Nico? Tell me right now!"

Then the yelling began.

I nearly shit out all my insides. My initial reaction was rage. What the fuck had my brother said to my mom, and why? What kind of shit was he in that he needed to blast my life to make himself look better? And how was I going to explain this to my mother? It was the worst fight we ever had. My mom started saying anything and everything stereotypical you could imagine a homophobic mother saying to her child. *You are disgusting. How many men? In my house? This is all my fault. What did I do wrong? You will destroy your career. You are an abomination.* Blah blah blah. And I fired back. I was in my new boyfriend's house throwing vicious daggers. I wasn't in the right place spiritually, physically, or emotionally to handle this like a reasonable human. I didn't even know how to handle it in my own life, let alone explain it to my raging self-loathing lush mother. So I disappeared. Again. Falling deeper and deeper. Spirits took over all that was left.

I didn't talk to my mother for months afterward. I destroyed my newfound relationship with the boy I had started dating. Bethany and I started arguing, like, for real; I was taking a lot out on them at the time. And once again I found myself desperately spiraling. I truly began to understand what it was like for an addict to need the bottle, need the powder or the pill, need the shitbag enabling friends, need the escape.

I HAVEN'T TALKED too much about what it's like to be an actor, even though that's what I do. Here's the thing—as an actor, if

you're going to do the job well, you have to *become* the character you're playing, to embody them. At the time, I was playing
a fucking serial killer on *The Following*, and part of his damage
was that he couldn't deal with the fact that he was bisexual.
Life imitating art, right? It's only in looking back that I can
see that I was killing the people around me—the people I
loved—with my drinking and drug use during these years. The
screaming matches I couldn't remember, the shit I did at parties while I was blacked out, the fights Bethany and I had that
were blurry for both of us. And all the shit Bethany had to put
up with because taking care of each other is what we do for
each other.

Bethany was an angel to me, yes, but the strains of addiction didn't only affect me. Addicts surround themselves with
other addicts, and they were partying with me more often
than not, enabling plenty of situations. We were debauchers
together, and both very messy at times. We sometimes got so
worked up in the heat of an argument that I would wind up
breaking glasses. Truly violent outbursts, the literal and meta-
phoric smashing of shit. We were broken, in abusive relationships with ourselves, until we healed in tandem over time,
holding each other up and holding each other accountable.

Bethany has struggled with their own addictions over the
years. But there has always been a key difference in our ability
to manage our behavior. Bethany had a job in fitness, working
at the studio, working on their body. They were always a better
addict than I was because they had to be; they didn't have the
time off that I did. They were able to wake up in the morning

and stop drinking, I wasn't. I didn't have to be at the studio at five in the morning, training people five days a week.

Bethany got me to work when I was too fucked up emotionally or hungover to get there myself; they washed the sheets or the floor when I pissed in the house. It was ugly. But I showed up for them in similar ways—picking them up at parties when they were too fucked up to get home alone, staying awake till the sun came up after too much cocaine and too many tears from recounting childhood traumas, and holding their hair back as they hunched over the toilet when it all got to be too much. And what still gets me now is how unnecessary all of it was. That's what I mean, in part, when I say I was born into the wrong world. There are lots of reasons the world hates on queer people, but what would it be like if none of us had to go through that shit? If Bethany and I didn't have to hate ourselves and feel ashamed of our desires for such a long time—and, also, if you're straight, how much easier it would be, for *you*, if you didn't have to go through this process of convincing yourself that it's okay for other people to be queer. How much better could we love one another and ourselves?

Anyway, the day before we shot the final episode of season one of *The Following*, the director called and told me that my contract was either going to be renewed for the second season or that I would die at the end of the episode. I wouldn't find out until we were actually shooting. My character didn't make it, but it was honestly a relief, albeit a temporary one.

Almost immediately after, I was cast in this mockumentary film called *Hunter&Game*, playing the role of a drug addict DJ named Carson. I showed up to the audition in a full-length fur coat and big glasses, having just smoked a blunt washed down with some honey whiskey. Carson was a good guy who happened to be an addict, which made him bad. It was perfect.

And then all hell broke loose. I filmed for a month super guerilla-style in the city. And I was blacked out almost the entire time. All of a sudden, I had reason to continue the party. It was for my craft. I *became* Carson. Partying nonstop, getting into trouble, asking a different Starlet to marry me on a bender; I almost blew up the apartment with a bonfire on the balcony one night, got thrown out of clubs, bought way too much cocaine, and so on. Watch the movie, and you will see me in full effect. It's an incredible performance, but that's the thing: I wasn't performing. That was my life.

Those months Bethany and I lived together in New York were a mix of light and dark, yin and yang. We were closer than we'd ever been, and we were both growing into ourselves, even though our drinking and partying were out of control. It's funny how sometimes looking back all we can remember are the bad times. I have to remind myself constantly that we did have a lot of great days.

I don't want it to seem like we were complete monsters. One saving grace was babysitting our friends' kid in Queens, totally sober, mind you. He was barely two, and we would spend full days with him playing house around the neighborhood. We'd take him to the park, me fully decked out in my front-pack baby carrier, and I would feel whole again. And I saw Bethany as both a mother and a father, juggling both energies and responsibilities effortlessly, and I fell deeper and deeper in love with them every visit. This little dude was like this ball of bright light, shining into our darkness, and also making the light between us brighter and brighter.

Bethany looked at me one day in the park while I had the little man strapped to my chest and said, "Nico, no matter how things turn out between us, I want us to have a kid together." There wasn't a question in my mind—never has been—that Bethany and I would be parents together at some point or another. We were made for it. But how we would eventually get there was still up in the air.

It was right around this time that Bethany told me they were a lesbian. They'd been working through years and years of religious guilt, and were finally able to admit their physical attraction to the same sex. I was still more comfortable identifying as somewhere under the bisexual umbrella, but where exactly was still unclear . . . shit, it still is. But Bethany was adamant about the fact that I would be the only "man" in their life from here on out. They wanted to really explore dating women seriously, not just having random sex. And I couldn't have been happier for them. I knew how much I had learned about myself from dating a person of the same sex and wanted Bethany to experience all it had to offer, the good and the bad.

And then, lo and behold, I was out of work again, which meant I would have to move back to LA to see what I could find. I asked Bethany if they wanted to come with me, but they needed to stay in New York. They had a career, and a new apartment in the East Village, and were looking for a first girlfriend. The night before I left, we got properly wine drunk, blasted Ben Harper's "Blessed to Be a Witness," and had sex on the floor of their new apartment surrounded by boxes and cowhides.

Afterward, we spontaneously decided to go get matching tattoos that read *blessed*. (This was way before #blessed became a thing, people.) For everything that had gone down in that year of us living together, nothing truly bad had happened. We were divinely protected. Celestially blessed. We both sort of knew by now that me living in LA would only be temporary, and chances were, I'd be back in the city soon enough. And no matter what, however steep the mountain ahead, I had my mustard flower to hold on to. No matter what, I knew I couldn't fall backward. Well . . . not completely.

## CHAPTER 5

A BUDDY OF MINE IN LA HAD THIS HOUSE UP IN THE HILLS OFF BEV- erly Glen Boulevard and Mulholland Drive. It was a turn-of-the-century Spanish estate tucked all the way in the back of a dead-end street, Chrysanthemum Lane. He had moved to New York and rented me the entire bottom floor. Right when the puppies and I got situated, I decided to start taking my life seriously for the first time in a while. I needed a fresh start all around. Sobriety.

I'm such an extremist that when I got sober, the idea of a relapse seemed so foreign. When I set my mind to something, I make it happen. Willpower has always been one of my strongest suits. *Free Will*, am I right? Sure, I would get the shakes for a couple of days post-binge, but I fought through. My willpower has always been next level. Really, really intense like that, no matter what.

The same night I made the decision to get sober from alcohol, I had to find a way to redirect my addiction. At this point, it had been years since I had created substantial art. I found solace in the blank canvas. It was a way to distract myself from the temptations of the spirit. For so long alcohol was a creative tool for me, a way to express myself through the fogged lens of reality. But sooner than later, it began to take over, and I was no longer able to see. I became addicted to blindness. But it was time to open my eyes again, no matter how painful.

I began with a lot of self-portraiture, shining lights on my addiction and current identity. Then I moved to a lot of really dark pieces. Imagery from crime scenes, death, homeless youth with needles in their arms, satanic rituals, decay, but all with this possibility of hope and transformation. In the four months that followed, I painted more than I have in my life. Dozens of pieces, small and large, three-dimensional, sculptures, even. At one point, I was even jerking off on a collection of paintings I had done of porn scenes reimagined and using my cum as varnish. HIGH ART. I felt whole again, isolating myself from the rest of the world as a form of healing. The magic bloomed again right there on Chrysanthemum. I was genuinely happy, healthy. Living off the sun, art, and self-love.

So much of what I do, what we all do, is about love. From love, for love, because of love, driven by love, gained and lost love. And every day, my definition of love can flip upside down, changed by the people who crawl into my heart and make it beat at a different pace. And not surprisingly, love has always been the one thing to break my willpower. Love is the only thing in my life that has ever gotten in the way of my committed force. Love is so many things, but it always, always, always makes the world new again. Creates another universe entirely. It opens up this portal from what you thought you knew into what you're discovering. It's magic. Infinite time travel. To a new place, new dimension, new country. New *you*. New *us*.

Which brings me to the night I met Gabriel. Other than Bethany, the greatest love of my life. The encounter was nothing short of spellbinding. I'd been sober for about four months, making art, feeling reborn, ready for *anything*. It probably wouldn't have hit me so hard if I hadn't been doing this work on myself. I was already broken open, heart exposed, working things out, repairing, ready to step through to something else.

It was a night like any other—the night before New Year's Eve 2014—and a friend called me to come to a party. I was like, "No, no party for me," and my friend was like, "No, bitch, there's someone coming out tonight, somehow you *have* to meet." I hated being sober in clubs and bars; what's the point? But I caved. Apparently there was this other energy pulling me toward something else, someone else entirely. It was crowded, dark, all these revelers getting ready to start the next year by forgetting the one that had passed, making resolutions they might never fulfill. I was this effervescent warrior ready to move through all the booze and drugs with my feet on the ground, knowing that I'd remember everything that had happened the next morning.

I found my friend immediately, and he took me up to a VIP room. He didn't have to tell me who the person was that I was supposed to meet. There he was across the crowd, sitting with a group of people, leaning back on a couch, drinking, smiling so hard I swear I could hear the sound of his lips creasing. As time slowed down straight out of a classic rom-com, so did his movements. He was elegant with an air of caution, like he was bearing some weight the rest of us would never be able to lift, but for him, it was easy. Just a part of who he was. I watched him stand on his seat and start dancing, captivated by the way his body moved. The way his hair flipped in the strobe lighting. And that soul-piercing smile. This pure, almost supernatural power, in the body of a mortal man.

I went to him as he moved like water on the leather booth and he looked down at me as if he'd been expecting this. Our eyes met, and before we'd spoken a word to each other, the portal opened. I was falling, as if I were seeing a million lifetimes all at once. I already knew this man, had known him maybe since forever, and now we were meeting again, continuing something that had already been happening in different lifetimes, different worlds, new dimensions. We didn't even exchange names right away. I asked him if we'd met before; apparently we hadn't. He raised a hand, and a few minutes later, someone brought me a drink. I politely declined and told him I was sober, and he seemed a little disappointed.

The club was too loud for us to really have a conversation. I remember shouted whispers in each other's ears, heavy breaths brushing souls, and the feeling that everything was happening in half time. At the end of the night, I walked him outside, and he gave me his number. His driver pulled up in a Bentley, and he told me he was flying to Vegas the next day to continue celebrating the New Year. "If you want to come," he said, "I'll send someone for you in the morning." He said this as if I had a choice. I think he already knew that I didn't. I said, "If you text me in the morning, I'll think about it."

I waited for the text from him as soon as I got home, and

the next morning it came through as promised. I called the regulars and asked them what they thought. Bethany was excited for me; they hadn't heard me this captivated by someone maybe ever, especially in my sobriety. They had started dating this girl, pretty seriously, for the first time, who would wind up being their longest same-sex relationship to date. Jamie was wary; Jean laughed at me and told me to go. And go I did.

Gabriel sent a driver for me, and I was whisked away to his private jet. Who the fuck was this man? I honestly had no idea. I had my bag packed with all the essential designer clothing, and as I rolled up to the tarmac, I saw him. Softer than the night before, even more beautiful. He was sober, unarmored, and a little nervous in a cute way. Which only made me more interested. We sat side by side on the short flight, as if we'd known each other forever. There was no small talk—everything went straight to the heart immediately. Childhood, hopes and dreams, all of it.

We arrived at the hotel, and headed straight to the presidential suite Gabriel had booked. I'd never seen a room of these epic proportions other than in the movies. A proper food spread was laid out, and a fire was already burning in the fireplace when we got there. In his room, out of the corner of my eye I saw a butler in the closet shining a row of already immaculate shoes. The huge closet was full of designer suits, as if Gabriel had already been living there. I ran my hands along their shoulders, lapels, seduced by them. I turned to the butler and asked, "Where did these come from?" The luggage and staff had flown on a separate plane, but I couldn't imagine anyone would travel with so much. The butler smiled at me without actually smiling, and I realized he'd seen this reaction before.

Gabriel came into the room, and the butler was dismissed. I was still standing in the closet, touching the suits. "Do you want to try something on?" he asked. *Duh!* I pulled a Givenchy leather jacket from the rack, straight off the runway, and tried it on. In that moment, I was whatever he wanted or needed me to be. I took him by his stubbled face, his skin a few shades darker than mine, his breath warm, and ever so slightly touched my lips to his. I knew not to give it all up too quickly, so I threw off the jacket and ran out of the closet all over again.

It was officially New Year's Eve, and that night, we went to the club for a Las Vegas blowout. I was all the way through the looking glass, forgetting myself and who I was—whatever happened, Gabriel would keep me safe. Living in this fantasy, my grasp on sobriety was getting weaker. I had only been sober for a few months, and all of a sudden I was in this alternate universe. Gabriel looked up at me and asked me to have a drink with him for New Year's, and I caved. Fell deeper and deeper into those hickory-smoked eyes, the right one with a freckle that seemed to always be watching. He hadn't asked me what I preferred, but he got the drink right, of course. A Don Julio 1942 on the rocks with a splash of soda. I didn't stop to think about whether I would drink it. He'd given it to me, so it was mine. I wanted to please him, right from the beginning.

On the dance floor, after so many tequilas I can't remember, Gabriel told me who he was, where he was from, and what it meant, as someone from a prominent family from a much more conservative country, for him to be there with me right at that moment. This desert ruby among diamonds, showing me all his crimson glory and imperfections. Yes, the glitz and the glam and the clothes and the money were great and all, but honestly I didn't care; this man was so much more special than anything material. This was divinely spiritual.

Later, I texted Red to tell him I was in Vegas and who I was with. Our lives were so crazy that this was something we often did. Checking in on each other while always throwing slight shade or one-upmanship. One of the benefits of being queer is that folks get folded into your family, if you're lucky, and you can tell them anything. Our Hollywood lives could get very surreal, and this was the most otherworldly experience I'd ever had. Like a dream I hadn't even known I'd been dreaming had become real.

Red has a sense of humor that goes on for days, and his response was so good that I had to show Gabriel. I wanted to make him laugh. But he didn't laugh—he got very angry, and said, "I thought you were different, but you're just like the rest. An opportunist." Cue my heart blasting out of my asshole and flying all the way back to LA.

Gabriel stalked away and we didn't speak for hours, avoiding each other in the club. I drank most of a bottle of tequila. I couldn't deal with having hurt him, this love I'd known for less than twenty-four hours, but also for lifetimes. Finally, right before the clock struck midnight, I got up the courage to approach him, to try to apologize. We went somewhere private, and he began to cry. "No one can know about me," he said. "You're a privileged, liberal, white American. You can't possibly understand all that is at stake for me."

I started crying with him, and promised that I would never hurt him, never put him in danger. I didn't say I loved him, though I knew this was already true. We both knew it. It was only because we'd crossed through that portal that Gabriel forgave me that night. Our love was bigger than any of it—the possibility—of entire worlds, whole countries, different whens and whys in time. And as midnight struck, while the deep club bass reverberated through our bodies and lights bounced off our spirits like a stellar collision, I kissed him once again. This time for real.

We slept in the same bed in his luxurious room that night. I gave myself up completely to him. I wasn't sure if I was ready to sleep with him, yet I'd always been ready. His magic, his force, made me feel, for the first time in my life, how I imagined it would feel to be a woman. I had a vision while he was inside of me, so clear that it was like we were there, transported from that room, maybe to the time and place where we'd first met a long, long time ago. Maybe Gabriel went there, too, felt it. This love changed my body, my language. It was after I met him that I started seriously writing poetry. He introduced me to Kahlil Gibran and my soul has been forever changed.

The next day we frolicked around Las Vegas, and in the evening took a flight back to LA. I had seen a glimpse of Gabriel's world in the States; it was time to show him mine, whether he liked it or not. I brought him straight from the airport to my house in the hills, a place I was very proud of. Highly curated with all the artwork I had created and the collection of treasures I'd gathered over the years. It was no presidential suite, but it was mine. And if he liked me, he had to like all of me. If he was at all uncomfortable, it didn't show. If I was at all nervous, it wasn't clear. We had the most normal, sober American night I could muster. We went to the movies, went out to eat, nothing fancy, and then back to my house to sleep. I lit a fire in the fireplace next to the bed and threw on some Lana Del Rey, and we collapsed into each other. And it was perfect. Exactly what it was supposed to be. A timely bloom on Chrysanthemum Lane.

Gabriel flew home the next day, and I was already at a loss without him. I needed to make this work, no matter the distance between us. We talked, for hours and hours on the phone and on FaceTime, and I began to understand how small some of my concerns were in light of all that was happening with him. In his conservative country, homophobia is rampant and crimes against the LGBTQ community are on the rise. He had to go back there and live in fear, knowing that he could lose everything; all I was really worried about was having fights with my family, drinking too much, or maybe being turned down for jobs. I had been so wrapped up in my feelings of guilt and shame, which were real and valid, but knowing the dangers Gabriel faced made me want to be stronger. This was the first time I started to understand just how protected I'd been all my life, how sheltered.

Love really changes everything.

Even though Gabriel and I were dating long distance, he asked me to be monogamous, and I immediately said yes. Honestly, I didn't have even the slightest desire to sleep with anyone else. He filled up my whole world, my imagination, my body. I had to tell Bethany immediately. They had begun to really establish themselves in the NYC lesbian scene. They were going to all the exclusive parties, had made a solid group of friends, and had changed their style completely. We were genuinely happy for each other. It was at this point that our relationship really started to shift. We were more than best friends, more than family. We were growing into our pride, something we had both struggled with for years. Bethany had come out to their family, brought their girlfriend home and everything. It didn't go that well, given their family's connection to the church. But Gabriel's situation demanded a new perspective from both of us. Bethany and I became even more protective of each other, constantly checking in to see how things were going, how we were feeling. How we were taking care of our mental health. But honestly, Bethany was more nervous about my decision to not be sober than anything.

I didn't go back to being sober after Gabriel left. That spirit was back, and I was just going with it, doing my best to ignore how dangerous it might be. I was going through a lot, being away from the person I loved and dealing with all the things knowing him was bringing up for me. I knew we could never be open to the world—not that I was ready for that, anyway, but it not even being a possibility was still so upsetting to me. Especially given my public persona. We talked about how he had only casually dated white men—classic American-looking beefcakes not unlike me—and this was the first time I ever thought about who we see on television and in movies, mostly, and how these images influence people all over the globe. Gabriel had some sorrow around the fact that he just wasn't attracted to men who looked like him. And I started to question why pretty much all my coworkers were white, and why the people at Hollywood parties were mostly white. And the producers and directors, the people who had the most power to make decisions, were even whiter than the actors I worked and partied with.

At this time, I still hadn't really made up with my mom after all those horrible things she had said to me after Rocco outed me. But it was time. Gabriel had broken open my world, filled it up with more love than I even knew I had, and all things with my mom needed to be forgiven. Ever since our fight, my best friend had been missing from my life.

So I called her. And she picked up.

There was silence.

And then I said, "Mommy, I miss you."

We both started to choke up on the phone, and I knew she wasn't crying because I might be gay, but because she knew losing her kid wasn't worth it.

"Nico," she said, "it's not you being gay or bisexual that hurts. That's not it. It's that we've always been so close. You tell me everything. But I found out from Rocco. You didn't come and have a discussion with me at all."

"I'm sorry, Mom. I just didn't know how."

"I've been sitting alone in my bedroom, thinking, Why wouldn't you just talk to me? Why wouldn't you just come out to me? I mean, don't you think I always had an idea?"

I sighed. Of course I did.

"The worse worst part for me," she said, "is that you weren't honest."

It's true. I talked to my mom about everything. I told her

about the first time I had sex literally two minutes after it happened, as my mom was staying in the hotel room adjoining mine. I told her about the first time I got drunk, high, cried, celebrated a role I'd booked—everything that's ever happened in my life, my mom was the first person to know. I needed my family, no matter what. I've always needed all of them.

"Well, Mom. Guess what? Since we're being honest?"

"What?"

"I have a boyfriend. He's the most incredible person I've ever met. And he's stupid rich."

This was language I knew she would understand.

"And I think I'm going to come out to the whole family. Do you think you can handle that?"

"God, Nico, why do you have be so extreme? Do whatever you want, just don't say a word to Grandma."

Holy shit. My mom and I had just had the most real conversation about my sexuality we'd ever had, and even within her passive-aggressive tone, there was resolution, acceptance. She knew she couldn't change me, so the next best thing to do was acknowledge me. I hung up the phone and broke down in tears from the weight of what had just transpired.

NOW, THIS WASN'T a lighthearted thing, coming out to my entire family. But I needed to. And not just for myself. I needed to for Gabriel. To show him I wasn't scared, and that even if his family couldn't know about our love, mine could. I wanted to show him that I could be strong, too, that I could take a risk. And I wanted him to know that I understood that what I was doing wasn't really a risk for me, not compared to what was at stake for him.

But I had to work myself up to this in order to be ready. In the meantime, Gabriel was coming back to the US for Valentine's Day, and I had planned an epic art project to show how I felt about him. I made these huge stickers that read NICO LOVES GABRIEL and plastered them all around New York City while I was in town for fashion week. I put them on street signs, subways, restaurant doors, sidewalks, the Williamsburg Bridge, literally everywhere. Then I took photos and made an art book to give to him. The most romantic thing I had ever done for anyone in my entire life—a gesture Bethany had always expected from me but never received. It's not as if I've never been romantic with Bethany, but I'd never felt like I had to prove my love to them with a grand gesture. Overt romanticism in the modern world is somehow related to femininity; men are supposed to keep their emotions close to the vest. Up until that point, I had assumed the masculine position with Bethany, but as soon as I was in a same-sex relationship where the distribution of power was different—where I was in the "feminine" role—this sort of awe-inspiring amorous expression manifested.

Gabriel and I spent the week together, and he and Bethany met for the first time. I had never been more nervous to introduce anyone to Bethany. They were my person, my family, meeting my boyfriend, my man. We all went out to dinner, two sets of same-sex couples at a four top, with Bethany and me sitting across from each other. It was the first time Bethany and I had ever been on a double date, so to speak. It had its awkward moments, as Bethany and I tried to embody our new positions and energies at the table. It's funny, when Bethany started dating women, they immediately became the person I was in our relationship: the more dominant, "masculine" force. And as I assumed a more submissive role in my relationship with Gabriel, it was a challenge for Bethany and me to stay true to our relationship while also staying true to our partners. But overall everything was going well, and since Gabriel and I were staying in this massive presidential suite downtown, we invited Bethany and their girlfriend to come stay in the guest room. I wanted Bethany to experience this opulence firsthand. And everything went amazingly well. We all had a mutual respect for one another, no matter how many worlds apart. Bethany and Gabriel couldn't be more opposite, and I occupied the space between their yin and yang.

When Gabriel went back home, I was left with my loneliness and all the old demons, missing him. He knew that I'd been sober when we met, but I don't think he really understood that I had a drinking problem. To him, I'd just been taking a break from booze. I'd never told him I was an alcoholic. I don't think that was something I could even admit to myself at that point. And he never saw my day-to-day life. We were always seeing each other in our little otherworldly bubbles. When he went away, the walls started closing in on me again. And now I had this new stress of coming out to my entire family.

I flew to Chicago to visit the brood soon after Gabriel left in February. My mom's sister, her husband, and my two older cousins lived across the street from the house I grew up in.

Grandma lives with them now, too. These dudes were my older brothers, or as close as you can get to brothers without having the same parents.

My older cousin is a fireman—that's the family business. His dad, grandpa, and great-grandpa were all captains in the fire department. Growing up, he was my idol. He had his hair bleached and his ears pierced. He was the first one in our generation to get tattoos; obviously, I followed suit. He has a sleeve now in memory of 9/11, a fireman looking up at the Twin Towers as they burn. He played guitar and bass and had a band that had gigs at my mom's bar. He was a hockey player, too, a really good one, and he dated pretty artist girls and wrote poetry.

His younger brother was closer to my age, so we spent a lot of time together. I had a lot of firsts with him. He used to drive me to high school in the mornings. He bought me my first pack of Camel Blue cigarettes, introduced me to hip-hop, taught me how to jerk off—you know, older brother stuff.

My mom's sister worked as a gym teacher for fifty years at an elementary school in inner-city Chicago—the other *other* side of the tracks. For as long as I can remember, she has been the voice of reason. If ever I had any sort of argument with my mom or grandma, I would run across the street to get her. As a teacher, she always had a way of navigating a dilemma—she listened, but as a gym teacher, she also knew how to yell when she needed to.

When I was in high school, she started teaching summer classes for elementary school kids—math, English, the standards. She asked me to assistant teach with her for two summers. It was incredible to be able to see part of the city through the eyes of these kids who were nothing like me. The experience probably taught me more than even attending my own school. The kids would tell us about not having food to eat, about drug use and gang violence, and for the first time in my life I saw a world outside the privileged bubble I had been born into. While my aunt was raising her own sons (and sometimes me), she was also there for all these kids, and they treated her like a queen.

So when she came to pick me up at the airport, I needed her to be there for me in more ways than one. Almost immediately I spit out the news: "I'm a bisexual, and I have a boyfriend." It didn't go well. She proceeded to tell me that all she had ever wanted for me was a beautiful wife and kids, though she did say she wouldn't treat me any differently. Just as we reached the house, I could tell that she was getting more aggravated. Her husband was outside shoveling snow—he could be straight out of an old Rodney Dangerfield movie—and when we pulled in, she told me to tell him. I said, "Hey, I'm a little bit gay and I have a boyfriend." My uncle is the coolest dude ever—his response was, "That's great, baby. I'm so happy for you." My aunt immediately snapped back, "*Gay*? You said 'bisexual' twenty minutes ago!"

"I'm still figuring it all out!" I screamed as I ran inside to see my grandma. I told her all about my new "friend," making sure to be extra cautious with my word choice. Then I went downstairs to tell my cousins, and all was well. They gave me some brotherly shit, but it was good-natured, assuring me they loved me no matter what. One weight after another was being lifted from my shoulders. I had officially told my family, apart from Grandma, and had this extra-cushiony security blanket of a rich boyfriend who lived halfway across the planet, so it seemed somewhat intangible to them.

Gabriel planned to come to LA in early spring to spend his birthday with me. He wanted to have a huge party, and I was suddenly in the position of finding a gift for a man who literally had everything. The only thing I could do was find something esoteric, one-of-a-kind, a gem in the overflowing boxes and stashes in my grandmother's collection. I told her I needed a gift for a friend, one who was very rich. "I need something special," I said, "something money can't buy."

My grandma, of course, thinks money can buy *anything*, and she took me into the vault where she keeps her gold, and gold only. There, I found a beautiful antique gold pocket watch. I knew when I saw it that it was absolutely perfect. But it needed a personal touch. I took it back to LA and had it custom engraved to say: *Whenever, wherever, I'll be there.*

Ugh, so romantic.

Despite the "relief" of coming out, I was still drinking more and more. I thought I had it under control. I was less in denial than I had been when Red and I were together, but I still had issues. And Gabriel had his own huge hang-ups, despite how in love we were with each other. I started to wonder if I'd ever be with a man who didn't hate himself for being queer. One of the ways Gabriel managed his shame was to never, ever bottom. He was always playing the "man" when we had sex, and he demanded that I act and look super masculine. As Starlet had been, he was uncomfortable with my femininity, especially in public, so I learned to hide it with him, too. At one point while we were watching *RuPaul's Drag Race* together on FaceTime, he even asked me if I was like "those girls." I said, "What do you mean, am I a drag queen?" He said, "No. Are you trans?" I laughed because I had never considered the possibility, but I was shocked that he would even ask me that in the first place. He proceeded to tell me that he couldn't be with me if I thought for a second that that could be me. This was painful, and a different kind of pressure—a gendered pressure—started to build and build in me.

Rocco's birthday is around the same time as Gabriel's, and I asked if he would consider including Rocco in the festivities. I've always wanted the best for my brother, and I knew the party would be epic. Despite him outing me, I couldn't hold a grudge. The love was too deep, and it hurt more to try to hold on to being angry at him than it had hurt that he had outed me. I more or less understood his reasons. Having grown up in my shadow, Rocco had felt the need to assert himself, especially since he was having a hard time getting his shit together in LA. For his birthday, I just wanted to show him a good time. And I wanted Gabriel to see what a magic sorcerer my brother truly is.

The thing is, when Rocco and I are together, things get crazy. He handles his liquor and drugs better than me. He's a machine, a beautiful human machine that I can't keep up with. We rented the presidential suite of a hotel, and by the end of the night the room was totally trashed. The whole night, Rocco and I were singing sulky blues and soul—Rocco has an incredible voice—with this girl on the piano. Later we instigated a full-fledged cake fight, and at one point Rocco even convinced the whole party to come outside on the balcony while he jumped from one ledge to another, thirty floors up. We were fucking idiots.

The next day, we had tickets to Coachella, and I had a massive hangover. I was sick and had the shakes, and I pulled a classic alcoholic move: I filled a water bottle with vodka. Amazing that alcoholics can be so in denial that we think this stuff doesn't have a smell or that no one will realize. Anyway, Gabriel didn't know I was a day drunk; he'd only see me drink when it was "appropriate." I was blackout drunk before noon, and at some point in the private helicopter trip to the desert, I gave Gabriel his present. I don't actually remember how it went, but I know it wasn't how I had intended it to go. How could it have? When we got to the house he had rented, I passed out on the bed, and when I woke up, he asked me if I'd been drinking.

"No," I said. "I'm just tired. From last night."

Why do drunks lie? It's the shame, of course. I knew, just by him asking, that I'd fucked up. But, just as with not telling my mom about Red, it's the lying and hiding that can be most painful to people. Gabriel found the water bottle, smelled the booze, and came back into the bedroom, where I was still trying to sober up.

He was furious. "How could you lie to me?" he asked. I could see how much he was trying to control his hurt and anger, and I felt scared. Not that he'd hurt me, but that not even he could protect me. And I knew there was no way I could protect him from *me*.

Then he said, "Whenever, wherever . . . Nico, you're right in front of me, and you're not here."

That went straight to the heart, and I freaked. "Fuck you," I said. "I was sober for a reason when I met you."

He was still furious, but he softened a little. "Are you an alcoholic? Is that what this is?"

This was the first time *anyone* had asked me this. And I started to rage. I don't even remember all the things I said to him. Anything I could say to push him away, to push away the truth that he was telling me.

*DENY, DENY, DENY!*


GABRIEL LEFT. We continued texting, but things felt broken. A couple of weeks later, I locked myself in my house and went on a days-long bender. Shit escalated very quickly. The doors to the house were wide open and a gaggle of friends came in and out of the revolving party. I wound up taking a bunch of Molly up my ass, smoking DMT, snorting cocaine, doing mushrooms, drinking tons of liquor—the whole kit and caboodle. I loved this human so much, and the only way I could deal with his not being there was to not be there, either.

After a solid four days without placing a single call or text to Gabriel (though I had a handful of missed calls from him), there was not a lick of alcohol left in the house, and I called Bethany.

"Baby, I think I need to go to the hospital."

"So go," they said calmly. And I did. The best thing that came out of that bender was that I actually knew I needed help, desperately. I was completely falling apart and had no grip on reality whatsoever. I wound up in a psychiatrist's office later that day in complete disarray. Hysterically crying but completely numb all at the same time. He gave me a three-day Xanax prescription to wean me off the bender, as well as Antabuse, a preventative drug that if mixed with alcohol would make me insanely sick, and a prescription for Wellbutrin, an antidepressant. Western medicine, y'all. But I was too far down the rabbit hole to look for anything else at the time. I needed help fast.

During that three-day Xanax comedown, I came to realize I had to break up with Gabriel. I selfishly blamed him for my drinking, just as I'd blamed Red. Classic alcoholic deflection.

The problem was that I was desperately in love with him. This, of course, is something alcoholics do—push away the people they love the most. I needed support in breaking up with him, so I called Bethany yet again for help. I decided to email him instead of doing it over the phone, but I couldn't write the email alone—fuck, I'd been strung out on Xanax for three days, barely able to feel anything. And when I called Bethany in numbed shambles, they showed up. My relationship with Gabriel had put a strain on Bethany and me, and I missed them. They felt my bender was directly related to my relationship with Gabriel, so they were more than happy to lend a helping hand. With Bethany's help, I sent an email to Gabriel, explaining that I'd been in a great place when I met him five months earlier—sober, eating healthy, working out, painting every day. But when I fell for him—hard—I wound up backsliding into substance abuse. And while I only had myself to blame for the decision, I needed to take care of myself first if I was going to be able to take care of anyone else in a relationship.

Gabriel wrote me back soon after. His response was calm, controlled, and also obviously deeply hurt. I'd been a coward, and he was elegant even in pointing that out. More proof that next to him, I was just a child, and a spoiled one at that. He could also tell that the email I'd sent him had been written by more than one person. His postscript was to guess that Bethany had helped write it, and he sent me this direct, disappointed reminder: *You have to take responsibility for yourself.*

I was obviously embarrassed, but as the twelfth Xanax was kicking in, I didn't have it in me to feel a fucking thing. Any type of benzodiazepine has the ability to make the rest of the world temporarily disappear. But I had accomplished what I set out to complete: my relationship was over. The greatest romance I had ever experienced had almost killed me. When the Xanax wore off, the idea of a broken heart really made sense to me for the first time in my life. Gabriel didn't break my heart; I broke it myself. And now I had to put the pieces back together.

SO LATER, after the hospital and the breakup and all that, I was missing my father. Missing him in a way that all the men in my life would never be able to fill. He was my first experience with abandonment, and though my uncle and aunt suddenly disappearing from our lives was fresher, this old wound had opened again, and I needed to see him. To heal something that I'd been putting off and pushing down for a long time. So I devised a plan.

I was heading to Chicago for the Fourth of July to see my family, as I do every year. I was turning over a new leaf for sure, and the antidepressants were working. But they also made me feel like I was invincible—so I flushed the Antabuse and started drinking again. I decided to call my older brother, from my dad's first marriage, to devise a surprise father-son reunion.

My older brother is pretty dope, and there is an unconditional love between us that is implicitly understood, no matter what. He also looks a lot like Elijah Wood, which I've never quite understood. He picked me up the morning I arrived in Chicago, and away we went, butterflies and all. It's not that I was nervous; I was just excited. I forgot what my dad smelled like, forgot his laugh, missed the Carmex, and now that I was older and knew more about myself, there was more of him to appreciate. As we pulled into the driveway, I couldn't run to the door fast enough. Like a bull in a china shop, I barreled through the back door and jumped into his arms. We both wept and wept and laughed and wept some more. He had no idea I was coming, but looked me dead in my eyes and said, "I knew you would do this someday, I knew you would just show up," and show up I did. We wound up getting hammered on vodka-Kahlúas, eating food with all the dipping sauces imaginable (my dad taught me the art of the dip eons ago), playing board games, and smoking menthols around the kitchen table. It was honestly one of the best nights of my life. And the craziest part of it all was the ways I saw myself in him. Those mannerisms I'd embraced are apparently hereditary. I am wildly in touch with my effeminate energies, and reconnecting with my father after all those years made me realize that I had adopted much of that from my father—the way he crosses his legs, the way his "fancy fingers" flare when he talks, the way he cackles. Word has it that his dad, my grandpa, performed in drag in the navy back in the day. Fact. This neon canary blood runs deep. It was like looking in the mirror that night. The nature and nurture aspects of our relationship had never been so clear to me. I am a product of him in ways I had never even imagined; some of my best qualities come directly from my pops.

I wonder if my dad, or really any of the men who raised me, would be as queer as I am today if he'd grown up in my generation. If he had had the knowledge, resources, and vocabulary, would he have been different? I wonder what my queerness would look like if my parents had stayed together, if it would have been easier having him in the house. I wonder if my dad is happier than other people because he doesn't need or want anything but what he has. Sure, he complains about money from time to time and has a bad back (apparently that pain is hereditary, too), but my daddy is happy, from what I can tell. He enjoys the simple things in life. He and his wife make pottery and sell it all over North America. We talk every once in a while these days, and it's nice. I wish things between him and my mom were cordial, but I realize they may never be, and that's okay. In so many ways, my dad is still a huge mystery to me. I don't really know who he is past what I see. And maybe he doesn't, either. And that, too, is okay with me.

It's interesting to note that when I am in a same-sex relationship, I am immediately transported to my issues of masculine abandonment. That feeling, with both Red and Gabriel, of laying my head on a man's chest. That smell of musk. The reek of supposed protection. Was it that I self-destructed and fled from those relationships to protect myself, to prevent them from abandoning me first?

I didn't hate my dad for leaving, I didn't hate my uncle for his unannounced departure, I didn't hate my mom for the way she treated my sexuality, I didn't hate Red, I didn't hate Gabriel, and I definitely didn't hate Bethany, Jamie, or Starlet. But I did hate this part of myself that succumbed to the spirits, and it was getting worse all the time.

## CHAPTER 6

WAS DEVASTATED AFTER GABRIEL AND I BROKE UP, BUT I DIDN'T really allow myself to properly grieve him, instead blanketing any sort of remorse with antidepressants and alcohol. I'm not sure I gave myself the room to really grieve any of my past relationships, so that hurt and loss lingered and built up. I just kept pushing through, going on with my life, partying and looking for work. Even the visit with my dad, which had felt so important, so healing, soon faded from memory as I succumbed to the spirits that were haunting me. One thing about drinking is that it doesn't allow you to move through your emotions. And that's kind of the point for an alcoholic. The quickest way to lower your vibrational force is to drink. In one way or another, alcohol has been used to keep people in a lower state of consciousness for thousands of years. I still wasn't ready to call myself an alcoholic, even as the pressures of my life kept intensifying and it was becoming more and more obvious that I wasn't able to deal with them. The common misconception about alcohol is that we think we're consuming it, when in actuality, it is consuming us.

Not long after I sent Gabriel the email, I booked the part of Josh on *Younger* and moved back to New York. I was living in a sublet apartment on Twenty-eighth Street, and it had the worst energy I'd ever felt in any place. It was drowning me. Bethany and their girlfriend had been seeing each other seriously for over a year, and when I wasn't working, we were all partying together. We started throwing epic blowouts, wrangling a solid group to join in on the debauchery, and one night a friend gave me some ketamine. I was used to blowing white powder up my nose at that point, so when I saw the lines spread out on the table, I was under the impression it was cocaine. False. Later, I stood in the hallway of my apartment building for what seemed like hours, trying to get the key in the door, and for the life of me, I couldn't. That was the first and last time I made that mistake. It was around then that I decided to start drinking and getting fucked up alone. I didn't feel like I could trust myself around people anymore. I didn't even want to be around people. That's how deep my shame was.

But ever since the fight I'd had with Ashton during *The Beautiful Life*, I'd sworn I would never let partying interfere with my work, and I didn't. I got into a routine of going on three- or four-day benders, going to a Korean spa to sweat it out for hours, and then doing the couple of days of shooting for the show each week. I would wake up in the middle of the night, hungover, and start chugging booze. My apartment had a fire escape that led to the roof, and I would go up there at night; for the first time in my life, I started having real thoughts of suicide. But even those thoughts didn't really touch me; it was almost like they were coming from someone else's body. That was how numb I was, completely numb, for the first time in my life. It was worse, even, than being in pain, angry, or heartbroken.

I would wake up in the morning and start drinking, knowing that I'd stay holed up in my apartment alone all day unless Bethany came by to check on me. They were really the only person I'd allow to see me in the aftermath. This is when Bethany really started noticing there was a problem. I started getting really flushed when I drank, like my body was rejecting the alcohol. When Bethany talks about that time, they say things like, "I started to track how you were drinking. How you were sneaking drinks when no one was looking, or how your eyes would begin to lose focus." For the most part I was pretty good at keeping my shit together and my behavior a secret, but Bethany always knew I was blacked out before anyone else did.

Bethany was maybe the only thing that really helped me get through it. But those mornings when I woke up and reached for vodka like it was coffee, to try to get drunk before all the shame and guilt set in, there was this part of me that was whispering, *This isn't you; your life is to love; your magic is your power; you have got to love yourself.*

It was like I was reaching out from six feet under during this time, trying things to get my body clean, even while I was pouring poison into it. I went to the spa, tried cupping and acupuncture, was revisiting old herbal remedies and super-food concoctions that I hadn't taken in years. I knew my old magic was still there, buried underneath the numbness. I just didn't know how to get it back, how to hold it in my hands long enough to actually do something with it. And even if I had, I can't say that I thought it would be worth it. I was mostly single during this time. There were a couple of short-lived relationships that don't even seem real to me now because *I* wasn't real. I couldn't bring myself to sleep with anyone. It felt like poison. I felt like poison.

THE NEXT COUPLE of months are a blur. I'll spare you most of the gory details. I mean, you get the point by now, right? But you do need to hear the story of my rock bottom.

It was December 2014, and shooting for the first season of *Younger* had just wrapped. The last scene I shot was when my onscreen girlfriend, Liza, comes out to me while on Ecstasy as being forty instead of twenty-six. My character on the show was a mess about the whole thing, and that didn't help things for me. After shooting, I went on a bender, and called someone from Craigslist to come to my apartment to do my hair while I was fucked up. Rocco flew into town and joined in on the festivities. I got motherfucking beyond culturally inappropriate dreadlocks. Don't ask me why. The whole process took seven hours, and that same night my brother and I showed up to the *Younger* wrap party totally obliterated. I'd never been really fucked up around any of my coworkers from the show. And I was showing up with this new persona—some douchebag white guy with dreadlocks—so unlike me that people didn't even recognize me at first. I still just needed to escape myself.

I ended up bartending the party, and the next morning I woke up with my scalp on fire from the tight locks. I screamed for Rocco to find the hair clippers. And in the kitchen, just like when I had chopped off all Starlet's hair, Rocco shaved my head. But not in a cute way at all. We were both hungover, maybe even still drunk, and I wound up with bald spots, holes in my head, and a bag of expensive-as-fuck multicolor dreadlocks. That was my last day in the sublet, and Rocco and I had planned on renting a car to drive down to Florida to see my mom and stepdad's new house for the first time. They had left the California life for tax-free, Republican, gun-toting Florida the month prior. So there we were, packing up the apartment, somehow managing to convince a rental car place to give us some keys, and starting the seventeen-hour road trip down south. Fuck my life.

Rocco and I were in Florida for two weeks, wasted the entire time. We got into epic fights with our mom, our stepdad, and each other. I ended up threatening to call the cops on all of them at one point—it was horrible.

From there, Rocco and I flew to California. I had to be in Pasadena with the cast of *Younger* for upfronts. In the television industry, upfronts are gatherings where television network executives preview their upcoming series for advertisers, in hopes that they'll buy ad space during the new shows. All the major advertisers and press attend. I was out there on *Younger*'s dime, and I took major advantage of it. My best friend from high school came out, and we started partying hard in the hotel room, draining multiple minibars. We invited tons of people over, and at one point someone hired strippers. Now that I'm thinking about it, the times I've been the worst, Rocco has always been there. I like to think I can handle partying the same way he can, so I'm always trying to keep up, but I just can't. And part of the reason for that is that Rocco is having fun, and wakes up in the morning with a million-watt smile, wanting to tell the stories from the night before. I wake up full of shame and guilt, convinced I've somehow ruined everyone's lives.

There were a bunch of up-and-coming actors, quite a few years younger than me, partying at the hotel, folks I should have been a role model for. I embarrassed myself in front of all of them, though I don't remember exactly how. I was a mess. At one point, I fell and hit my head really hard, and pretty quickly everyone left. The party was over. When I woke up, from the bottom of my soul I wanted to die. But I just kept drinking alone in the hotel room. I was supposed to check out that morning, but couldn't. I actually couldn't leave the hotel. I was trapped there, and didn't know how to get out. I remember stalking naked around the room, slamming my head into the marble walls on purpose. The walls had literally closed in on me as I sprawled on the bathroom floor surrounded by piss and blood from where I'd hit my head. I managed to call Rocco to come help me, to get me out of there, and when he showed up and found me, he went into panic mode. I was so far gone that later he told me that I pissed on him while he was trying to get clothes on me. He still talks about it to this day as the worst he's ever seen me, even throws it in my face when I bring up his addictions—"I'm not as bad as you were, Nico!" I racked up a bill of more than a couple thousand dollars and wound up getting scolded by the network for my behavior. I said I would pay for it; they wouldn't let me, but told me if it ever happened again, there would be a problem.

I had a flight back to New York that night, for the *Hunter&Game* premiere, and I packed a bag that had one sock and a T-shirt in it. I went from JFK straight to Bethany's apartment and crawled into bed with them, hysterically crying and shaking, and they took care of me. My mustard flower. Somewhere along the way, I had lost both my wallet and my phone. Living the Hollywood dream, y'all.

I knew I was beyond repair when I woke up unable to stop shaking my head. I was screaming, "I can't stop doing it, can't stop doing it, can't stop doing it." And I wanted it to be done. That was it. Fucking done.

YOU'VE MAYBE HEARD that AA cliché "sick and tired of being sick and tired." That's what happened to me. I never went to AA past a couple of meetings, though I think it's safe to say I've been going through all the steps in the last four years, and writing this book is one of them. Bethany and I went to the premiere of *Hunter&Game*, the film where I'd played Carson, the drug addict DJ. I had three tequilas that night because I had the shakes from withdrawal, and I said to Bethany, "This is it. I'm done with this shit."

The next morning, I went to see Jamie, who had been living

in New York for years and running a raw food restaurant in the West Village. I got a full seven-day arsenal of juice cleanses from her place. I also bought a copy of *A Course in Miracles*, which is an everyday affirmation practice. And it worked. Finally, for real, it worked. I've been sober from alcohol since that morning. Thank all the Gods ever imagined. I have to tell you, I'm so fucking grateful I'm done writing about this period of my life. I have found myself spiraling even just finding the words to make sense of it all. It's so much easier for all of us to just forget and never have to relive any of the shit we've done, but that was never an option for me. Not then. Not now.

Alcohol is what led me to all the other chemical-based intoxicants, and alcohol has always been the spirit I had real issue with. Cannabis, for instance, was a spirit I never really battled, so I didn't have to let it go. I call my sobriety "fluid" because I still use cannabis and other plant medicines. Everyone's recovery is different; there is no right or wrong way to get sober. For me, it's about staying healthy and maintaining control. Most of us are under the influence of *something*, whether it's caffeine, chocolate, marijuana, or any number of over-the-counter or prescribed medications. Very few people aren't using anything to help them get through. I haven't overcome my issues with addiction—I have just substituted healthier choices for the truly toxic relationships, the poison.

A week later, I moved back to LA to find more work, as I had no idea what would happen with *Younger*, and the professional coast-hopping cycle continued. It was good to be back in California, the land of sun. My numbness had gone away, practically overnight, the second I got sober. I had honestly wanted to die, and now I demanded to live. My emotions came rushing back, and they were amplified. For a few months I went raw again, did yoga every day, started listening to myself intensely, remembered who I'd been when I first moved to LA. I started making so much art out there; I had to make up for lost time.

When I look back on it now, I can honestly say that sobriety is what birthed my queerness as I understand it today. Life was too short, and suddenly, I had no fucks left to give. I no longer felt held captive by the limitations of Hollywood. The interplay of fame culture, materialism, and addiction are so obvious to me now. When I was able to really be myself, it felt less important to be the person they wanted me to be. I needed to figure out who I actually was underneath it all, because the ways I'd been halfway hiding had almost killed me. I rediscovered the wisdom that storytelling can be a way to heal, and I started making and telling the real story of myself. My physical appearance started to change significantly. I dyed my hair a new color every few days, got my nose and nipples pierced, got more tattoos. There is something undoubtedly queer about taking ownership of your body. Tattoos and body modifications, as forms of art, are vehicles for storytelling. A way to journal our experiences permanently. In this world's power structure, one that wrongfully dictates our bodies are not solely ours, tattoos and piercings have the ability to mark individual property. I started wearing whatever queer-looking shit I wanted to premieres and press interviews. I wasn't technically out publicly, but my appearance changed so drastically that my team totally flipped out and told me I was going to ruin my career if I didn't tone it down. At one point they even hired a press coach for me just to cover their asses.

This was 2015, y'all, the same year the United States finally legalized same-sex marriage in every state. Just let that sink in for a second.

Not the wrong body, but the wrong world.

Instead of listening to my team the way I had when I was twenty and cut off all my hair, I said fuck it. I went on the *Playboy* radio show and talked about sexuality and gender, though I didn't officially come out. To try to understand my own story, I started documenting my own life in a serious way, filming almost everything. I had come up with this plan for a documentary, and *NICONICONICO* was born. *NICONICO-NICO* is an expression. An evolution of my artistic existence. A lifestyle brand. An unpredictable beating heart. A way to organize my curiosity, and I'm a pretty curious dude. I filmed the documentary with my brother in LA. It opens with me getting NICONICONICO tattooed right above my hoo-ha and then follows me for twenty-four hours in LA while I'm existentially spiraling. Everything that had been in my spirit just became art. I was healing myself through storytelling, becoming myself all over again. Rocco had told me he'd stopped drinking as well, but he started showing up to work drunk, and the project fell apart.

In only a couple of months, I looked very queer, was being perceived as queer, and had started thinking as queer. Suddenly, I wanted to know more, to get educated, to learn queer history and language. The history of my people, of who had come before me, and who had, in a lot of ways, made me who

I am. I started having real discussions with my friends and people I looked up to about navigating a queer conversation publicly.

The first person I called was my friend Jeremy O. Harris, who's this radical Black queer playwright artist extraordinaire, a person whose life experience was entirely different from mine. But he's a wickedly smart, flamboyant mad genius and I knew he would have an answer to just about anything. We sat in my apartment for hours as I asked question after question. How the fuck did we all get here? And what do I do with it now? He really started me on my queer education. He told me who to follow on social media, which journalists to be reading, which movies to watch. We talked about everything I thought I knew and everything I didn't, and weighed the pros and cons of publicly coming out. Jeremy began to tease out of me the things I should say and the things I shouldn't. He encouraged me to begin to use my voice for change only if I was up for the commitment—"This isn't something that just happens and is done, Nico. This is forever." Obviously, I'd been dating all kinds of men up to this point, but my understanding was really limited. I'd been operating in this kind of closeted/half-closeted mode, and my relationships with men had ended in part because I hadn't been loud and proud about who I was.

Then I started dating a bisexual queer man. He also dated a lot of women, but he wasn't trying to hide and pretend he was heterosexual when he was with a woman. He was always unapologetically queer in the way he acted and the way he looked, not ashamed of anything, and he actively didn't want people to think he was straight. *Why the fuck would I want that?* was his attitude. I wanted to know everything. And not just the shit that had already happened. I wanted to know what the world hadn't imagined yet.

FOUR MONTHS AFTER my sobriety and my transition (yes, that's what it was) into queerness started, my team sent me the script for an HBO show called *Mamma Dallas*, written and directed by Mike White. It was a show about trans women and drag queens living in Texas. I don't think the script would have been sent to me if I hadn't started being who I actually am, and reading it blew my mind. I'd never seen a project like it before, and I wanted it more than any other part that had ever come to me.

Casting wanted me to read for one of the queens, but after I read the script, it was the closeted redneck boyfriend of one of the women that I wanted to play. I figured I could work a lot of shit out doing this. And I got it. I flew to Dallas to shoot the pilot. As it turned out, my friend La Démi was in town for Beautycon with the trans trailblazer Gigi Gorgeous. I'd first met La Démi in LA when she was only sixteen, already fierce and ferocious on the scene. That was before she had started to really transition, and even meeting her then, I never thought of her as having been born male. It just didn't make any sense. She was this Latina bombshell with enough bleach, spray tanner, and makeup to blend right in with all the LA girls. We were at a party once, just after I met her, and I flipped on her friends for still using *he/him* pronouns to refer to her. I remember us cuddling on the couch, and I looked her in the eyes and said, "You know, we're gonna be best friends forever."

We hadn't seen each other or talked in years, but the fact that she was in Dallas at the same time I was shooting this pilot was just crazy, and I was elated to spend time with her. I picked her up from her hotel one rainy afternoon, and we went antiques shopping. I'd been shooting, and I was in full-on redneck drag—boots, hat, jeans, really getting into the part, wearing this costume full-time around Dallas. I'd been surrounded by queens, trans women, and nonbinary people (I didn't even know the word *nonbinary* then) for a week, and I was really feeling myself, coming into my own in the part of this closeted character as the real me was working on finally coming out.

Bethany had lived in Dallas for three years, so I knew there was this big rodeo in Fort Worth. Somehow I convinced Démi, Gigi, and a gaggle of girls from the show to jump in a truck and head to the motherfucking Texas rodeo. Fort Worth is about as Texas as you can get. And the stockyards and rodeo show is where the people gather. The building is more than one hundred years old, and the people who attend are exactly who you would imagine. This is the heart of America; the blood is about as red as it gets. Two hours of bronco riding, bull riding, calf and cattle roping, barrel racing, and trick lasso, with me in full cowboy garb and a crew of the queerest, hottest people you've ever seen. Everyone clocked us; we obviously stood out amid all the Wrangler, Stetson, and Walmart. And just as the entire stadium stood up to cheer, Démi grabbed my hand and pulled me down next to her, and in that sea of cowboys, we were just a boy and a girl staring into each other's eyes. We both leaned in at exactly the right time, hidden from the rest of the world, and ever so softly we shared our first kiss.

To our surprise, most of the people were actually really great. Taking pictures with us, telling the girls they were beautiful. A few older men got really nervous and said some shitty things, but there were enough of us that it wasn't a real problem. The courage it took all those femmes to show up in a place like that was unprecedented. I was able to be a bystander and hide behind this hypermasculine male drag, but to witness this crew unapologetically being their queer selves in a stereotypically unsafe space was fucking epic. It was fuel.

On the way back to the hotel, La Démi reached over and grabbed my hand. It was a really beautiful moment. Not necessarily romantic, just us saying that we wanted to be there for each other. To hold space for each other. And that is exactly what La Démi and I have done.


*MAMMA DALLAS* DIDN'T get picked up, which is the greatest heartbreak of my career so far. It was just a year or two before its time. (And this is even after Joe Biden announced to the country, in 2014, when he was still vice president, that the trans rights movement had reached its "tipping point.") HBO wanted *Mamma Dallas* to be campy, but Mike was like, "No, this is about real people, with real lives and real emotions." And HBO ditched the show.

But the greatest thing that came out of the experience for me was La Démi. We started hanging out a lot in LA. She was heavy into the party scene, so I wasn't going out with her—sobriety stuck so hard, so good. But I lived in downtown Hollywood, and she'd come to crash at my place after a night out. The first time she came over, I was like, "Hey, I'm too soon into sobriety to have sex with anyone." La Démi looked at me and said, "Honey, that is not what is going on here. No, no, no, ma'am!" Then she looked around at all the weird trinkets and art and the altar in my apartment and said, "By the way, bitch, this apartment is trans as shit. You are trans, baby, when are you gonna realize it?"

Of course, we wound up sleeping together for the first time about three days after we said we weren't interested. It was like after it was off the table, we were free to explore it. It was absolutely some of the most incredible sex I've ever had. La Démi hadn't technically started a medical transition yet, but sleeping with her was more like sleeping with a woman than sleeping with any designated-female-at-birth women had been. Her feminine energy was cosmic—like, the embodiment of the divine feminine. Something far outside or beyond the bullshit of socialized gender. It was this divine awakening for me.

It's important to note here that one DOES NOT need to medically transition in order to be trans. I repeat, a person DOES NOT need medical intervention in order to be recognized as trans. Every person is entitled to their own journey, no matter what it looks like.

La Démi had lived her whole life with no fucks given, and she was the first person I was truly intimate with, whom I loved, who lived a queer life so happily. She wouldn't be anything other than who she was, and I'm not sure it had ever even occurred to her not to be herself at all times. She started to medically transition soon after we began dating, and I wound up going to her doctor's appointments with her to see how the estrogen shots were administered. I became fascinated with the ability to chemically reshape our bodies in order to feel and look more the way we truly felt. This way of being trans was no longer just something I'd heard about. It was a big part of my life. It was this person I was falling in love with.

Démi is never on time and likes her ego where she can see it. Démi eats, sleeps, and breathes beauty, fashion, organization, dreams, life, and the gratification of not knowing what's going to happen next. She says "she" is her pronoun because society has chosen to see things and assign labels. I knew I wasn't like her—well, not exactly. I wasn't born in the wrong body. But maybe she wasn't, either. Maybe she was born in exactly the right body, a caterpillar turning into a butterfly.

Démi taught me that in a perfect world, there are no limits. *Maybe there are no pronouns. Démi is Démi. Nico is Nico.* Gender didn't have a hard meaning in Demi's life. *Boy. Girl. Man. Woman. Gender fluid. This. That. Trans.* Like it is for so many of us, those words never totally made sense to Démi. I wanted to learn as much from her as I possibly could. Absorb. Exchange. We took each other under our wings, and we were inseparable. It was right around this time that I decided to brand my chest with tattoos. I had the words NOT THIS. NOT THAT. BEYOND DEFINITION. spread across my collarbones with the Mars and Venus (male and female) symbols on each end. I was ready to literally wear who I was on my chest for the world to see. Even in Démi's feminine transness, there was a fluidity to her expression that far exceeded the physical, that was ultimately *beyond* gender. I began to embrace the word *fluid*, which to me has implications that aren't confined only to gender. It can be used to describe the spectrum of nuance and color between many dichotomies. Celebrities like Miley Cyrus and Cara Delevingne had started using the word publicly, and it made a lot of sense to me. *Not this. Not that. Beyond definition.* Men and women. And even more so, the space between.

La Démi was my public date at the time, and there were lots of photos of us in the press. Photos that my mom saw. Of course, she flipped out. She called me up and said, "What the fuck, now you're dating a tranny?" I clapped back: "MOM! We don't fucking say that word anymore. And NO!" I didn't tell her then that we were together; I was too focused on figuring myself out to deal with the bullshit from her at that point. I didn't want to fight with her, not with my best friend in the whole world. My mom thinks I'm after what she calls "the freak show." That I just want to be more and more extreme, as intense as I can be. But, Mom, this is just normal life, and because I love you, I want you to understand this. We have families, jobs, dreams—we go to sleep and wake up in the morning. The real freak show is thinking that some people aren't actually people.

Nothing could stop Démi and me, or so we thought. Then, La Démi's father passed away. She found out lying in bed one morning in my Hollywood apartment. I was there for her in her grief as much as I could be, but when someone really close to your partner dies, it takes a massive toll on the relationship. We decided it would make the most sense to stay in each other's lives as best friends. She was still so young—we both were. We had so much more of ourselves to figure out. Part of why her father's passing was so difficult was because her dad never got the chance to meet La Démi in all her glory. A week later she showed up to his funeral dressed as who she is—a woman. That's what I love about her: no matter what, she shows up. That is fierce as shit. And Mom, it's also TOTALLY FUCKING NORMAL.

WRITING THIS BOOK, I came to some profound realizations regarding my middle school years. In 1999, when I was in the seventh grade, my principal came out as trans. Yes, you read that right. In my somewhat conservative, sheltered little Midwest bubble, my middle school principal publicly transitioned from male to female. I spent quite a bit of time in that principal's office when all my popular bro friends started giving me shit for being your typical jock turned thespian. There was even this one kid who threatened to kill me on AOL Instant Messenger. So my mom was constantly at my school, demanding the administration do something about it. She's always been a pitbull about defending Rocco and me.

Anyway, our principal was very obviously *other*. Before she transitioned, she had this long wavy hair and spoke in soft, gentle tones. Just before eighth grade started, everyone got a letter in the mail from our principal, saying that she would be returning that school year as a woman after having both top and bottom surgery. The letter was detailed in a way that wasn't anybody's business. But I get it. This was way before the trans zeitgeist, and she wanted to answer the questions, no matter how inappropriate, before anyone asked them. People freaked out, and a few families moved out of the school district. My house was shocked, flabbergasted, even, but we didn't move. I kind of vaguely knew what was going on, but only because I'd seen trans people on *Jerry Springer* (I was too young to understand how fucked up those representations were). I just felt kind of curious about our principal. It didn't occur to me to think there was anything wrong with her. But the people around me definitely thought so.

As I started to learn about how the world we know is ordered, and how everything is connected, I began to realize more and more just how much I was taught to hate people of different genders, sexualities, and races from the beginning. Taught to hate all those differences all at once. By my family, at school, through the media, by my friends. I was programmed to hate everyone not exactly like me—white and male and straight and upper-middle class. I always felt resistant to this programming, but of course, it got into my psyche anyway. It gets into all of us. And we're never supposed to see past it. That's what ideology is: thinking that what people have taught us is actually reality. But really, it's just a bunch of made-up shit that only serves the folks who already have most of the power in the world.

Now I can see that at the same time my family was telling me to hate people, they were also telling me not to trust my intuition. Telling me that the ghosts and energies I was seeing and sensing weren't really there, to the point where I tried to convince myself that they weren't. I've always wanted to believe in more than what was right in front of me, always wanted to find a way to see past this world and into the next. I don't think it's an accident that I was being taught to deny my intuition at the same time I was being taught to hate Black people, queers, and so many other kinds of people. Kids have great bullshit detectors. Which is probably one of the reasons my mom and grandma were always telling me to shut up.

SO IT WAS the summer of 2015. I had just moved back to NYC to start shooting the second season of *Younger* and I was feeling great. Myself. New. And then I got a call from Gabriel. Out of the blue. My heart sank to my asshole. We hadn't said a word to each other since our breakup over email. He told me he was moving to New York and wanted to see me.

Fuck.

I'd been sober just a few months the first time I met him, and y'all remember how that ended. But I also knew that I'd left him in a shitty way, and I needed to make up for that, somehow. I met him for coffee in Madison Square Park. Anyone who's been to that park knows it holds some sort of magic. Smack-dab in the middle of the Flatiron District, it's a park full of history—fountains and trees and people and dreams.

As soon as I saw him, everything else fell away. I'd never fallen out of love with him, just pushed my feelings as far down as I could. From the second we saw each other next to the fountain on that warm day in August, it was on again. I had to put a lot of work into the relationship, and I did everything I could to win him back. It was all under the umbrella of making things right with him, making up for being a fuck-up, for breaking his heart. He was giving me a second chance, and I was determined to make it up to him any way I could.

But I wasn't the same person I'd been when we'd first met. My gender expression had already started transitioning. After getting sober, I'd not only started dressing more queer, sometimes going out in dresses or androgynous clothes, but I'd also started working on my body in a serious way. One addiction to the next. I was working out like a madman, sometimes twice a day, taking human growth hormone, testosterone, getting totally jacked. I had stopped drinking but was still filling the void with other substances. There was something about seeing firsthand how Démi's body changed that inspired me to take the next steps in my own life. In my own way. I had this intensely masculine body showing through my flowing fairy ensembles. It was like I was trying to live out both gender extremes at once. *Not this. Not that. Beyond definition.*

It made Gabriel uncomfortable, to say the least. I think it's fair to say that he hated it. Gabriel was just coming to terms with living in a new country with new friends and being gay, and here I was taking everything to the next level. Gabriel also had serious problems with my friendship with Bethany, even though we hadn't slept together in years. I suppose part of the issue with Bethany was rooted in him knowing that they had helped me write the email I used to break up with him. Bethany had the same serious girlfriend, and he never wanted to hang out with them, which was a major sore point in our newly rekindled relationship.

Dating Gabriel this time, I started to realize that what I

truly wanted in a partner was someone I could come up with and build a life with. Living with him, I didn't have to work for anything. It was almost like using a cheat code in a video game: after that, it just isn't as fun anymore. I was slowly but surely becoming a kept man, and that was dangerous for me. I didn't have to fight for anything material or work for my dreams and goals. I was always going to be the assistant coach to his head coach. We both knew this. Gabriel even said it to me directly.

Six months into us dating again, Bethany and I flew to a friend's wedding in Chicago. Gabriel showed up at our hotel unannounced, a true act of love and jealousy all in one. I slept in his room the first night he was there. The second night, he asked me to make a clear choice between him and Bethany. He was embarrassed, I was embarrassed, and I can safely say I've never seen Bethany more broken in my entire life. It's not as if Bethany and I were planning a romantic weekend at the wedding, but this event was something special for us. Our best friend from college, someone we'd met the same day Bethany and I met, was getting married in the same city. It was a throwback vacation for all of us. And it's not that I didn't want Gabriel there—I did. I wanted more than anything for everyone to get along. I wanted him to love Bethany, and I needed Bethany to see him in the same light that I did. These were the two greatest loves in my life, and I was desperate for them to get along. I can't believe I'm about to make this analogy, but . . . if Will ever brought home a dude who Grace didn't like, it wouldn't work! It was just too much for everyone.

I asked Gabriel to leave. He knew it was the right thing to

do, as much as it fucking destroyed us. That was the beginning of the end of our second go at it. And not a day goes by that I don't think about him. I still think about that pocket watch I gave him, and what I had inscribed on it has a new meaning for me. *Whenever, wherever, I'll be there.* Maybe not in the physical way I had intended originally, but energetically, a piece of me will always be his. And a piece of him will always be mine. It's like once you build that bridge in such a profound way, it never really burns. That energetic connection is everlasting. And even if it's not in this lifetime, Gabriel, I'll find you again.

The night Gabriel left, I slept in Bethany's room. It was the night of the wedding, and Bethany and I were lying outside under the stars, smoking a cigarette. Right before we headed to bed, I felt the presence of her dad and said, "Your dad's here, baby." Bethany's father had passed away when they were just ten years old, but they had never really had any closure or good-byes. So we went upstairs and were lying in bed when they started hysterically crying about the whole fiasco with Gabriel. I was attempting to defuse the situation. The TV in the room was off, I swear to God it was off, and the remote was next to it, far away from both of us. All of a sudden, the TV turned on to a Christian channel, and the hymn "How Great Thou Art" filled the room—it was Bethany's dad's favorite song. I never knew that before, and it was the first time Bethany had heard the song since leaving the church. Sometimes you hear old songs like that and you know every single word to every verse and every emotion that comes with it, no matter how much time has passed. Bethany started singing, softly at first, in complete shock, and the TV started flickering. They sang louder, crying harder; then the song ended and the TV went black. And that was that.

It was like Bethany's dad was showing up to show us we were exactly where we were supposed to be. The sign we both needed. We had been on such a roller coaster for almost ten years, and this was a really important angelic validation. It was right around this time that Bethany and I started calling each other Mom and Dad. Some people think that's weird, but it makes sense to us. It's like the spirits of our future children were begging for us to cement our relationship in new ways. And this affirmation from their own father took it all to the next level. *How great thou art.*

## CHAPTER 7

HOLLYWOOD IS A SURPRISINGLY INSULAR PLACE. I DIDN'T NECES-
sarily know how much or how fast the world was changing before I started connecting with people on Instagram.
There were suddenly all these people's stories, portraits of their
lives, all these queer and other kinds of people showing how
beautiful they are, and also how terrible they are. It made the
world so much bigger and my personal existence smaller; it
was also a massive catalyst for my education. The world is obviously still pretty fucked for queer and trans people facing
adversity and danger in their everyday lives, yet news outlets
still aren't reporting on it. According to the Human Rights
Campaign, a national LGBTQ advocacy organization, more
murders of trans people were recorded in 2018 than in any
other year, and the majority of these were of women of color.
Meanwhile, queer representation and visibility in pop culture
is more prevalent than at any other point in history. How those
two facts can exist in tandem blows my mind. It's like all we

care about are drag queen death drops, not when the girls out here are actually dropping dead.

At the same time, social media has made the isolation less isolating, and Instagram has been a big part of collapsing the traditional borders of geography and cultural access. You can find connection with your people, your chosen family, your community, your tribe, no matter who you are or where you live. Nowadays, national polls tell us that more than half of folks under twenty no longer identify as straight. Every day younger generations are rewriting terminology for identity expression. Partly because of the social media revolution, people are waking up more and more, telling their stories, and kids are realizing they don't have to try to conform to these traditional ideas of gender and sexuality.

Instagram was a big part of my healing process once I got sober. It became a much more personal journal than it had ever been for me before. I posted photos of the art I was creating, the new people in my life, and, yes, photos of myself. *A lot* of them. Self-portraiture, if I may. My changing body and my progression into sobriety as art. In a very tangible way, I was showing the world my process of coming to love myself again, and I was reaching out, through the platform, for connection. I wanted people to see me for who I am, and I wanted to communicate not only the difficulty of getting sober and dealing with my shit, but also the *joy* of coming into myself as queer. I was finding so much inspiration from all kinds of people I'd never met, and I wanted to give that inspiration back. I was starting to come full circle, getting back to that young kid who wanted to make the world better, who had all these spiritual ideas of love and connection.

Instagram is how Kyle and I found each other. Kyle is a social media celebrity, a "cewebrity," one of the folks who was using the platform as a way to make incredible art out of his life, himself, his body. For him, taking photos of himself is a ritual, a way to heal by telling stories about himself. Kyle is an unapologetic homosexual and was *nine* years sober at the time we started talking. He was sober, totally sober, and his presence was so fun and sexual and hot. We had mutual friends and ran into each other at parties throughout the years. I was usually drunk; he was not. I always had the biggest crush on him. The juxtaposition between his hypermasculine body, face, and style, and his effeminate voice and mannerisms made so much sense to me. And when I finally wound up getting my shit together, I reached out to him and said, "Thank you so much for what you've done on this platform around sobriety. It's really helped me."

We started DM'ing all the time after that. Flirting like crazy. We developed our own way of talking to each other that was almost childlike. It was very obvious from the get-go that we were both interested in seeing where this could go. But Kyle said he wouldn't be interested in me until I'd been sober for a year. It was too much of a risk for his own mental health. This guy was for real. He had his shit together, and enough self-respect—and respect for me—to wait until the right time for anything to happen between us.

Fast-forward a few months to New Year's 2015, right before my first anniversary of sobriety. I wrote to Kyle to ask what his plans were, and invited him to New York. And he booked a ticket. Just like that. I was throwing a New Year's party for a group of friends, Bethany included, and I wanted him to be my date. I had already told him all about Bethany and what they meant to me, and he seemed comfortable enough to give it a shot.

When he first came to my apartment, I was totally nervous, in part because our relationship online was already so intimate. And it was even scarier because we were both sober. There was no booze or drugs to mask our feelings. Kyle was maybe even more nervous than I was; he was so shy that he was shaking. He's so fucking cute when he's nervous. He came through the doorway in his all-black Nike ninja get-up, doing some sort of nervous dance and a voice with a lisp to break the ice. I hugged him for the first time, our hearts pounding against each other. We were both already so invested in this going somewhere that we could hardly talk to each other. I took him by the face and kissed him as hard and soft as I could, and from that moment, I knew he was going to be important.

The thing that I love most about Kyle is the difference between his online persona and his real-life demeanor. It's no secret that Kyle is an Instagram thot, constantly hypersexualizing himself and his body while also landing some of the best dad jokes imaginable. And in the real world, his energy is somewhat contrastive to his social media presence. We tend to think we know what people are into sexually based on what they look like or what they sound like. It was so interesting to have built up expectations from our online relationship after months of discourse through the small screen, jerking off to the idea of him hundreds of times. And then to have him right in front of me, a boy, coy, humbled. There was something innately feminine about his sexuality. I took on a more masculine role with him. And I'm not just talking about topping or bottoming. It was something energetic. Something I wasn't totally used to in dating men. And I cherished it.

THINGS ESCALATED BETWEEN Kyle and me really fast. (I know, okay? I'm seeing the pattern, too.) We started making lots of YouTube videos together. Kyle already had a pretty big following on YouTube and Instagram, and I was excited to collaborate with him. I hadn't publicly come out yet—meaning I hadn't actually *said* the words to the press—but these videos Kyle and I were doing are some of the gayest shit anyone has ever seen. We were falling for each other hard, and simultaneously filming ourselves to post.

A few weeks after we started dating, I hosted Gay Ski Weekend in Aspen and brought Kyle with me as my personal groomer. Kyle is a wizard hairstylist, and I convinced the team at Ski Week to fly him out with me. We never actually came out as a couple until after we broke up, but after posting pictures of ourselves waking up together in bathrobes, him pouring me coffee, social media and the tabloids really started asking questions.

I didn't really care. I was having the time of my life. Though, I suppose I did care on some level, because I felt as if I wasn't allowed to publicly admit Kyle and I were actually dating yet.

And for someone who was so out and so proud, I know that this took a toll on him. Even though this was 2016, it was a different time to be out in Hollywood than it is even today. But without Kyle, I wouldn't be where I am in this conversation or in this community.

At the same time, my creativity was exploding, spreading outward in all kinds of ways. Part of my queer education was figuring out how to express my queer self, my queer life. I started writing outlines for scripted shows. The documentary project I'd started with Rocco had never been finished, but it had given me a taste of wanting to tell my actual story, to keep exploring. I constructed a deck for a scripted show called *sexual*, which was based on my life, with characters based on all my friends and lovers. Needless to say, the show was queer as shit, and incorporated a lot of thoughts about gender. I took it to my agents and managers, and they were all stunned. They'd been freaking out at this point because of my appearance, but by sending them this not-so-fictional scripted outline, it dawned on them that I'd just come out. Officially unofficially. Cue the panic attack. Now they were really worried about what this would do to my reputation, my career—my ability to make money, in other words. And I get it—their job is to protect me.

How's this for a transition? Okay, so I've been obsessed with *RuPaul's Drag Race* for years. I don't really get nervous around celebrities at all. But in 2016, if I was in a room with a drag queen? I was fucking giddy. So one night I was with Bethany in Sticky's Fingers, a chicken finger fast-food joint in New York City, high as balls on the marijuanas. And who walked in? Milk. *It does a body good, girrrrrrrrrrl.* Milk was my all-time favorite queen from season six of *Drag Race*, because she was different. A quirky-dirky art queen who bent the rules on masc/femme expression. So Milk walked in, out of drag, and I grabbed Bethany and whispered, "That's Milk, that's Milk." Mind you, Bethany was high, so they were very fucking confused. We got our chicken fingers and ran out, too chickenshit to say anything to Milk. But that's what is so amazing about social media: five minutes after we left, I sent Milk a DM. *Spotted in Sticky's Fingers. I see you.* And it was on from there. We started chatting back and forth almost immediately and set a date for the following week to put me in drag for the first time for real. And it was everything. Almond Milk was born.

Getting in drag with a real established queen is a lot different from just throwing on some frock and a lip by yourself in your house. It is taken very seriously. And I was obviously a natural. I became a different person in full drag. All of a sudden, my ultra-femme mannerisms were celebrated; they had a place. Milk and I had a real friendship blossoming, and he and Kyle got along great. We started spending a bunch of time together, spitting queer theory, contemplating gender politics, and really getting into what visibility and representation meant on television. We started dissecting the acronym LGBTQIA, and at one point my entire living room was covered in Post-it notes as we began developing an unscripted sketch show on the queer community. It was heaven.

So there I was, sober from alcohol, with an amazing, hot, talented boyfriend, an incredible new queer drag queen muse, a steady job on *Younger*—my life was fucking good. But my career always has a way of throwing deeply emotional curveballs.

THAT SPRING, I was cast as the lead in an off-Broadway play called *Crude*. I played the role of Jaime, this capitalist, psychopathic oil company heir who's going crazy because he's worried the family company is going to go under. The character is a callous prick who doesn't care about the millions of gallons of oil his drilling operation is spilling into the ocean. He's a drunk, drug-addicted lunatic in a heteronormative relationship. It was almost like the devil was coming back to wave his finger in my face. Or maybe his dick.

Stage-acting is way more intense than doing it for a camera. The audience is right there, and part of performing is building and maintaining a connection with them. At the same time, the audience has to entirely disappear. There's no director to call "cut," no second takes. For two hours, you're really, truly someone else entirely, if you're doing the job right. And, of course, there were the weeks of rehearsals to help me understand this dude's psychology so I could get inside his head, which means he also got inside mine.

I'd been living super clean since Kyle and I had been dating. I'd even stopped smoking tobacco. But almost as soon as I started rehearsing, I bought a pouch of organic loose leaf and started all over again. In secret. It was the first red flag. The other weird thing that happened was that while I was playing the part, I started to wonder if I actually wanted to spend the rest of my life with a man. I was in love with Kyle, but I began thinking about the women in my life more and more. Bethany, who in so many ways really was my "wife"—we belonged with each other—even though we weren't sleeping together. I started thinking about having babies, and as the pressures of playing this super-cis heteronormative douchebag took a toll on my mental and physical health, the responsibilities of my gay relationship were becoming harder to grasp. The system, everything I was trying to fight, was tearing us apart.

I knew that I needed to be really honest with Kyle about everything. No more breaking up with people over email. We walked together over the Williamsburg Bridge, and as the sun was setting, we hashed it out. As we hit the halfway mark, I looked at Kyle and said, "Okay, we're four months in. I think we owe it to ourselves to check in. Where are you? How are you feeling?" Communication wasn't really our strongest suit, but we'd gotten exponentially close in such a short amount of time. I'd witnessed Kyle produce and perform his TEDx Talk about addiction and sexual abuse the month prior in North Carolina, and I don't think I've ever seen anyone so raw and unhinged in my entire life. Nor do I think he had ever had someone show up for him like that before. We were basically living together—him, Luna (his 125-pound mastiff—rest in peace, baby), and me, all in a loft apartment in Williamsburg. We had created this little family in such a short time, but I wasn't sure it was the family that made sense for me longterm. So I told him.

"I think I want a girlfriend."

The ultimate smack in the face for any gay man dating a bisexual. And I'm so sorry for it. Kyle, I'm so sorry I didn't ever tell you I loved you while I was dating you, because I did. Every single step of the way. I still love you. And I wouldn't trade our precious time together for anything.

I had Kyle on my podcast a few months later to discuss our relationship and breakup. But before I get to that, let's talk about the podcast.

*THE.*

*LOVE.*

*BOMB.*


IN AUGUST 2016, I got to work on *The Love Bomb* for real. Maybe the networks weren't yet ready for a television show about gender, sexuality, love, and polyamory, but I needed a bigger platform to share all my ideas about this stuff. I wanted the whole world to know there were so many different ways for us to think about love, and the podcast was my way of doing this. The idea was pretty simple: I would interview all kinds of people, whom I love in all kinds of ways, and we'd talk about what love and sex mean to us, how we express it, how it's always changing. In a journal entry from before the podcast launched, I wrote:

> *I'm doing this podcast for the sake of love. Love is spirit. Love is bodies. Molecules constantly crashing into each other and forming opinions. Manipulating memory to form instinct. But what we were taught only influences what we do, it doesn't dictate. Love is unconditional. No matter what.*
>
> *This is me spitting words into a microphone. REALLY*

*talking to people. Some who I've loved, love, or have yet to love. Vibing. Feeling all the good love feels. Choosing love is a way of life, the only way of life. I'm not necessarily a writer but I have words. I'm not exactly a poet. I am poetry. A teller of stories. This is a journal. A scrapbook. An audio platform. An energetic collection of emotional data. A sing-along love song. An explosion of love. And let's be honest, the world needs it right about now.*

I had never listened to a single podcast before I started recording my own. Maybe that's what actually made mine so special. One of my good friends from Chicago, Will Malnati, had made a name for himself in New York and had just started a new venture in the podcast space. At Will Radio was his podcast network, and he was hungry for new material. I had been a guest on one of his shows that summer, and pretty immediately after recording, he asked me if I wanted my own show. I obviously had a lot I was exploring, a lot I was willing to discuss, and it made perfect sense. This was a way for me to blast these conversations I was having in my waking life into the ether and share my education with people. This was it. My first real public step into the community.

We started recording episodes like crazy without really knowing what we were creating or how it would be perceived. The first episode I laid down was with Bethany, of course. Then Milk. Kyle was number four, and then the list just took off. I was in love with the platform. I could sit down for a few hours and have these deeply intimate conversations with people in my life, some of whom were my lovers, some of whom were friends, some of whom were people I looked up to. *The Love Bomb* began to take on a life of its own, and what it ultimately wound up creating was something I'd never dreamt of. For me, for my career, and for my people. My community.

So Pride in New York—it's a march, not a fucking parade— happened right around the same time I was getting *The Love Bomb* up and running, and I went out to party. The sober way, of course. At some pink-washed gathering at a West Village restaurant that night, I spent a long time talking to this one guy about all the stuff that was filling up my mind, my various obsessions. The podcast was fresh, and so were the discussions I'd had. I talked about fluid sexuality and questioning the gender binary, the spectrum of gender we all live on, and how I've dated and loved people who exist on all different points of that spectrum. I was talking about emotional connections with people and being fluid in my desires for people and connection.

Not exactly news, right? But it turns out the guy was a reporter, and the next day it came out in Page Six that *Younger* star Nico Tortorella identifies as "sexually fluid."

Over my morning coffee I got a Google alert on my phone— yes, I have a Google alert set up for my name, calm down. I clicked on the link, and saw parts of the conversation I'd had with the guy at the party the night before. Things like:

> *I've never been in any sort of closet ... I was never really in the house ... I think it's one thing to hide ... and it's one*

*thing to come out of the closet in a public statement ... But I've always done me and never been shy ... and have been vocal about it.*

Oh bitch, I nearly threw my computer off the balcony. But after a moment to process, I was able to reconcile and consider this my first "public" coming out. (I've had a few of them.) At first it was a disaster. My publicist called me at the crack of dawn in a panic, attempting to defuse the situation—i.e., kill the story—to no avail; and honestly, I saw that as a good thing. The item in the paper took the weight off my feeling the need to do any sort of major public coming out. The whole point of doing the podcast in the first place was to open the gate to have more conversations about the very ideas I'd unwittingly told the reporter. This was the perfect way to introduce *The Love Bomb.*

*Yes, I'm fluid. And now we're going to talk about it.*

It also helped the situation that I had started dating one of my good friends, a female. Now, I'm not going to get into all the details about her, how the relationship started or how it ended. But I will tell you how it brought Bethany and me even closer.

So for the past maybe seven years I had only been dating cis men, with the exception of La Démi. Bethany was really cool with it. And Bethany still to this day hasn't had sex with a "dude" other than me since Brooklyn. This has been a subject of a lot of conversations regarding our nontraditional relationship and its complexities. It's like if I am with another person who has a vagina, Bethany immediately feels uncomfortable, and part of this is because there's a chance I can get that person pregnant, which would undoubtedly affect my and Bethany's future. I love vagina, always have. I love dick, too. Fuck, I love everything! But if, for whatever reason, Bethany were to fall for someone who looks like me, or has the same parts as I do, I don't know that I would have an issue with it. I mean, maybe I would have to work through some shit at first, but I could get into it. And I think that's one of the biggest differences between our respective jealousies.

So around that time, there was a very clear difference between Bethany, the new people I was falling in love with, and the people I was sleeping with. But as soon as I started not-so-casually dating a cis woman (another starlet, here we go), everything changed. All of a sudden, it was an issue. (And speaking of issues—my own issues—around this time I did an interview with *Vulture* where I made the following statement: "Ultimately, in my fluidity, at the end of the day I never could see myself marrying a man . . . I could never see myself having kids with a man. I don't even like hanging out with dudes for the most part." This is the worst thing I've ever said publicly. Period. I was still so blinded by the construct of binary gender that I found it appropriate to feed into the great divide by making some erroneous general statement like this.) Anyway, I'd already started having very preliminary conversations about families and marriage with the other woman I was dating (I know I'm ridiculous, okay?), and it took a huge toll on my relationship with Bethany. Bethany and I have always talked about having kids. *No matter what.* But if I was dating another woman who had the potential of carrying my child, what would that mean for Bethany and me? Needless to say, everything was moving really quickly. And this other girl laid out an ultimatum. She told me that if we were ever to get really serious and have kids, under no circumstance would I be able to have kids with Bethany. A sentiment I understood . . . However, I asked her, If Bethany were to wind up in a gay relationship, I would of course be the person to donate sperm, right? Her answer: No. Absolutely not. Truth be told, at the end of the day, I respect her decision.

Ultimately, this was what drove us apart. But it did bring Bethany back into my life in a major way. Now we were forced to have new conversations about our future and our family and our sex lives. We still weren't sure what the future would hold, but we knew we would never put ourselves or our partners in a position like that ever again. And guess what? Bethany and I started sleeping together again for the first time in more than three years. It was like the first time all over again. Soul storm.

As I was having these public conversations about bisexuality and fluidity, I was sleeping with two different women over that period of time (Bethany still identified as a woman then). And I would be lying if I said having the safety net of an opposite-sex relationship didn't make publicly talking about sexuality easier. That's just how our patriarchal, heteronormative, homophobic system is built.

But *The Love Bomb* allowed me to publicly discuss sexuality and gender with my people, myself, and my God. Part of my being sober and being queer is this facilitation of connections between myself and other people, and this really began to come out in my work on *The Love Bomb*. And very quickly I realized that any sort of understanding of yourself that is deemed different from the rest of society is inherently spiritual. A connection with God, the universe, Allah, Jehovah, Yahweh, Jah, Buddha, the Almighty, whatever you want to call it. This is the foundation of all the personal and interpersonal healing work I am doing now, this intersection between myself, others, and the divine that wasn't possible when I was in Hollywood and only focused on myself and fame. Fame when wrongfully approached is false spirituality, false divinity. But when used for the greater good, the platform becomes one to spread awareness.

*The Love Bomb* went on the air in September 2016, and eventually became the number one health podcast in the US. Over three million downloads! Suddenly, people from all over the world were reaching out to me, asking questions about sexuality and gender. And young people, especially teenagers, were getting in touch to thank me and to share their stories. They also wanted advice, about how to come out, how to deal with their emotions. And this changed everything. I would receive thousands of messages a week from all around the world. I now had a responsibility. I had been working on other people's projects for so long, but now I had my own baby, of sorts, which was really helping people in major ways, and really helping me make sense of my own eternal purpose.

Then, a couple of months later, total disaster. I was in LA to shoot a spread for *PAPER* magazine. It was November 8, 2016, a day that will go down in history as one of the most miserable for the country. The news came in early in the morning. Motherfucking Donald Trump had been elected president of the United States. I shut down. I couldn't stop crying, and my brother couldn't understand why I was so upset; politics don't affect him, which only makes him more privileged and annoying, and only made me more mad. I got in the car to drive downtown for the *PAPER* spread and I was shocked to see how dead the streets were. Literally no one was out in Los Angeles. But in New York, protests were raging, people were filling the streets, and the moment I saw this on the news, I knew NYC was my forever home.

I got to the shoot and was elated to be surrounded by other queer people to wallow in the misery of the day. We supported one another, cried together, and laughed as a form of healing. A form of medicine. But it wasn't enough medicine. I needed to experience something new. I needed to leave the country, escape our impending doom. I know it sounds dramatic, but that's what it felt like at the time. And I don't know if it feels better today or actually worse. But I had to go. So I jumped on my phone the next day, and in fifteen minutes, I had a plan: I found the highest-rated ayahuasca retreat center in the Amazon that had availability for the holidays and booked a trip to Peru. It was time to heal. The medicine was calling.

## CHAPTER 8

TWO THINGS HELPED ME REALIZE I WAS READY FOR THIS JOURNEY in the Peruvian jungle. The first was that whatever we have inside us that we don't bring out will turn inward and hurt us. Destroy us, even. My aunt and uncle set me on this path of becoming a healer through healing when I was a kid, and I knew that my way of doing this was through story. But I had stopped telling stories, and when I did that, I forgot my own, and that had plunged me into darkness. I would go to Peru to travel through my own underworld, to understand what I'd spent years hiding from myself.

The second thing is that kids, every single one of them, are miniature sages. They are closer to the source of creation than we are, and they live in a state of amazement, in love, in wonder, with all they see. But they are slowly taught to stop appreciating, stop noticing, through socialization. And they are taught to hate. The people I love most in the world—my family— taught me to hate as a by-product of their love. But through the healing process of coming to understand the ways in which we were hurt, we can stop these cycles of oppression and hate, by coming to love not only ourselves and one another, but all of creation. Our ancestral curses can, in fact, be broken. It's a process of continual rebirth, and to be reborn means a part of us dies each time. As part of the healing process, we travel through our own underworlds to give these parts back to the earth, to bid them farewell.

It's said that to heal from trauma, the first thing you have to do is tell someone your story. You need to say it in words, to have a witness to it. You need to have someone *believe* you. Back in the late seventies, lots of LGBT folks started publishing their coming-out stories through independent or feminist presses. The people who needed them found a way to get ahold of them, through community networks, bookstores, gay bars, word of mouth. Those stories are messages from a different time, folks speaking out and saying they were human, too, no matter what history had tried to make of them.

There's so much more representation of queer and trans folks now. We need to see one another, to see positive representations of ourselves reflected back to us. People's lives are at stake, both their physical safety and spiritual well-being. I didn't entirely know what I was doing when I started *The Love Bomb*, didn't know how deep or powerful the platform could be. I was following my intuition. But nothing happens in a vacuum, and we don't get *anywhere* by ourselves, despite what the "personal responsibility," pull-yourself-up-by-your-bootstraps machine tries to tell us. We *always* get where we get with the help of more people than we can count, more people than we can even be aware of. I'm talking about our families and friends, the people who love and believe in us, and I'm also talking about so much of current white wealth being a direct historical result of slavery, and how *any* piece of property that is owned in the US today has in its soil the blood of millions of North American indigenous people. Healing isn't just about ourselves; it's so much bigger than that. It's about coming to terms with history, too, because history is what has made the present we're living in right now. This is history. This is our future. And it matters.

In the fall of 2016, right before Trump got elected, I started watching this show called *Gaycation*. In it, Ian Daniel and Ellen Page travel all over the world, meeting and getting to know various LGBTQ folks, and each episode tells their stories—their hopes and fears, the perils and oppressions they face, and the joy of culture and resistance they create in dangerous environments. Watching the show made me think more about what I wanted to do with storytelling and my podcast, and about how powerful it could be. So many episodes of *Gaycation* ended with me in tears, suddenly knowing about the lives of people in situations I would have never imagined, and feeling myself changed. Relieved of some of my ignorance, which is both scary *and* liberating. Watching that show made me want to dig deeper, to know more and to use my privilege and platform to seriously advocate for queer and trans people. And even deeper than advocacy, I started thinking about how to actually *change* the world.

On the podcast, I was having very public conversations with God. And I'm not talking about the old white man in the clouds—I'm talking about the God who lives within and connects all of us, and my voice and the voices of my guests were the particular expression of that singularity. There's something about blasting your thoughts and inquiries into the ether without knowing who exactly is tuning in that is inherently of God, to God, for God, and because of God. The podcast was about love, and in some ways, maybe I was trying to have a public conversation *with* love, to see what love itself had to say. I was putting out so much, asking the universe for manifestations of change and insight, for clues on how to take what I'd started and make it more effectual. Without realizing it, I was asking the universe for Ian Daniels to come into my life, conjuring his very being. And Ian came to me, so hot, hot, hot, and immediately changed my whole way of being and seeing.

Ian reached out to me in a deceptively light way, sliding right into my DMs: *We have the same chest hair, you and me; I think that means we should be friends.* The technological spark that lit the way. I had him on *The Love Bomb* a few days after that for our first face-to-face interaction, although it defied anything human. He came into the studio and read a poem he'd written for me. I had gotten used to writing prose for each guest, offering a spoken-word gift of appreciation as a way to break the ice and delicately tear down the wall between guest and host. Ian was the first to return the favor. And his words sucker punched me straight in the gut. Here are a few passages:

> *What will we be at the end of this, Nico?*
> *Will I get beyond the glitter of you?*
> *Past the good looks?*

*Will you even be able to tell?*
*You, the Hollywood heartthrob*
*The heart-shaped nose*
*The heart like a soldier in military training*
*Making heart-shaped bombs out of your electric air*
*Me, the boy who's willing to die*
*Me, the blast, me the bruise,*
*Me the head always at war*
*Us*
*Could we be the battlefield on fire that they watch ignite and*
    *burn with real flair?*
*But I do wonder, Nico*
*How good is your vision out of that lazy right eye?*
*Is there a limit to your sight?*
*By the end of this, will we look out past what we can actually see?*
*Past the outskirts of infinity*
*Can we help each other get beyond this motherfucking skin?*

*Maybe you'll tell me that in the real world you don't fit into a*
    *box.*
*You're neither this*
*Not that*
*You're beyond definition*
*You are beyond language.*
*Maybe I'll say let's*
*Intertwine our tongues*
*Create our own*
*Maybe you'll tell me you'll touch tongues*
*But not for the sake of words*

*Words fail*
*Words destroy*
*What do we do when we are tired of talk?*
*Maybe I'll say: we float*
*Luckily you're like water, Nico, even though your element is fire.*
*I'll build my raft onto your slippery back, grab on, glide so fast*
    *we die,*
*We rise.*

This, from a person I'd never met, but who saw me, knew me. I started falling for him immediately right there in that sound booth while we were recording the show. You can hear it in my voice, how deep in I'm getting, from minute to minute. Ian talked about his activist work over the years, what has made him who he is, and every word he spoke, I wanted to *do* more and more, to inhale everything I'd never known or thought about and become this positive force against the Trump regime. For the first time since the election, I felt a little bit of hope and possibility, a sense of what my role could be in turning back the rising tide of hatred in America. We wound up getting dinner after we recorded, a first for anyone I'd had on the show. We continued our conversations off-air, really getting to know each other. We took the train out to Brooklyn, where we both lived, and as I said good-bye and kissed him on the cheek a few seconds too long—it was on. With all this in mind, four days after recording with Ian, I got on a plane and flew to Peru, where my life would begin all over again.

. . .

I'D TRAVELED ALONE BEFORE, but this was my first time out of the country solo. I knew it was the only way to approach a trip like this. I'm very protective energetically of my people around me. The last thing I wanted was to be forced to put anyone else's experience before mine. This was my trip, in every sense of the word.

I packed light, just the essentials for a shamanic jungle immersion. After taking two planes and a motorcycle taxi, I arrived in Iquitos, the gateway to spirit. The city is electric, like a rundown power plant built at the beginning of the industrial revolution, untouched for decades. The streets reek of trauma, hope, healing, and the stench of meat from the Belén market. I made my way through the city's long alleyways in search of local tobacco. In most ancient indigenous cultures around the world, tobacco has been used as a form of medicine. In the Western world, we associate tobacco with addiction and lung cancer. A lot of the tobacco in Peru, known as *mapacho*, is an entirely different plant from the one we use in North America and is hand-rolled and unfiltered. I bought enough for the week to come and a few other essentials. I felt like I was in another universe entirely. And the real excursion hadn't even begun.

The locals in this city, once colonized by the Spanish and slowly being gentrified all over again, all know the white folks are here for plant-medicine reawakening. Ian had debriefed me on the ramifications of such modern-day colonialism. He challenged me on everything from day one, demanding I question my participation and reconcile the complication of attending such a ceremony, given all the arguments against cultural and spiritual appropriation by a gaggle of mostly middle- and upper-class white folk, who travel from all over the world to sit in the *maloca* (the sacred space in which ceremonies are held) and drink the holy indigenous brew, while the healers sing and chant in Icaro, their native tongue. Furthermore, the white people opening countless retreats in the Amazon often hire local Peruvians to run and facilitate these programs. The complex issue surrounding the cultural, economic, societal, and ecological impact of the ayahuasca retreat boom in South and Central America is a real one, and Ian forced me to stand face-to-face with my involvement. Nonetheless, I was there, wild-eyed and ready. I had needed to come; I felt it deep down.

I checked into a local hostel where the people from the retreat would pick me up the following morning. That night, I met a few Americans who were just returning from their immersion and gathered as much information as I could about the retreat center. It was very apparent they had been changed forever by the experience.

The following morning, about twelve of us—a group of people from all walks of life (yet all white) who would soon become my family—gathered in the hostel lobby to board a caravan. We made our way to a small fishing town and got on a boat for a two-hour trip down the Amazon. On the boat, I met our healers for the first time. I made sure to sit close to them to start communicating in any way I knew how. My

Spanish is wonky, but I could get by. Within thirty minutes, the elder healer reached into his bag and offered me a handful of mushrooms for the trip ahead. When a healer offers you a handful of psychoactive fungus, you take it, no questions asked. I knew this was the beginning of something so much greater than I could have imagined. As our boat made landfall and my foot touched soil, it all sank in: what was I actually about to get myself into?

Ayahuasca is a master healer to some, a master teacher to others. I've even heard some say that ayahuasca does not do any healing at all, but instead shows you what needs to be healed and how to heal it. In the Quechuan language, *aya* means "spirit," "soul," "corpse," or "dead body," and *huasca* means "rope" or "woody vine." The brew consists of two plants, *caapi* vines and *chakruna* leaves, cooked together to make a thick, tart spirit in which they magically combine to create the neurotransmitter DMT, a chemical naturally produced in our bodies that's released in high doses when we are born and when we die, and in low doses when we sleep. Many tribes and healers have their own mythical tales explaining how and when ayahuasca originated, but its discovery is most commonly attributed to the Shipibo tribe well over two thousand years ago, although work with the medicine exists in various parts of the world. All three of our healers were Shipibo.

The following testimonies, which I encourage you to read with an open heart and an open mind, are based on my limited firsthand encounters with a few healers, and in no way speak for all Shipibo. Furthermore, ayahuasca is a very powerful spirit medicine, and as a student of the master plant, I have the utmost respect and gratitude for the wisdom I have gleaned from it. I have been in ceremonies over the years with dozens of people and no two have similar stories; the medicine affects everyone differently. And no two ayahuasca journeys have been the same for me, either. We all bring our own set of circumstances, and the experience shows us who we are and what needs to be cleaned within us. The magic is born of the marriage between the brew and the God-given life force inside each and every one of us.

So there I was, in the middle of the Amazon jungle at a retreat center with all new faces, sleeping in a hut, being introduced to new types of medicine like *kambo*, a tree frog secretion that is burned into your skin, and *rapé*, a sacred tobacco blend that is snorted, all while preparing for my first of four ceremonies. I knew I was supposed to be nervous, but I wasn't—I was ready.

On the first night, after an hour or so of *palo santo* cleansing and silence in the *maloca*, I was invited by the healers to kneel before them as they offered me a shot glass of the strongest psychoactive on the planet. After they blessed the ayahuasca by blowing on it and chanting, I took the dose of thick, fermented-tasting medicine, bowed in gratitude, and retreated to my mattress on the opposite end of the room. For the first couple of hours, I felt like I had a handle on everything. Like I actually understood this medicine and its accompanying geometric visions. And I was just a little bit disappointed. I'd wanted to see something new, to access my subconscious and see what it had to tell me. I'd wanted to get *underneath*, to lift up the skin of my own world, to get to that deep reality where we are all sharing the same spirit and experience of a reality that is normally washed away in everyday life.

The healers had announced earlier in the day that we could have another shot of ayahuasca if we wanted, so I opted for a second dose. Right after the medicine was administered, I looked down at this white piece of cloth I'd tied to my wrist earlier in the day as a form of protection—from what I didn't know, but I knew it would mean something. This is the way of many of the trinkets I collect; they become sacred objects, holding meaning, language, and spirit, like bread crumbs I drop for myself along the path toward my destination. I looked down at the bracelet, untied it, and threw it behind me, into the darkness. And that was the moment when I lost control, when the medicine started to take me on the journey I'd come for. The bracelet had been me protecting myself, but it was time to let go, to see what would happen *without* protection.

They say that tobacco and ayahuasca are what brought healers to all other plant medicines, and that first night, I had a vision of a spider taking me through the jungle and showing me this particular root. The spider told me that there was a medicine that could help my eyes. I've learned to hide it as best I can, but I have a lazy eye—the muscles of my left eye have always worked at less capacity than those of my right. And when I was a kid, my right eye was always tearing up from a blocked tear duct; I had nine surgeries, and it was never fixed. I also have allergic shiners, which are dark circles under the eyes. That whole first night of the ceremony, there was this giant dark figure standing to the right of me, but I couldn't look over to see what it was. It was just there, hovering, impenetrable.

After the first ceremony was over, I went to the healers and the medicine woman to tell them about my vision. They assured me that this was exactly how the medicine was supposed to work, telling me they would try to find the root to help heal my eyes. The medicine woman prepared juice from basil, and squeezed it into my eyes each day for the rest of the week that I was there. It burned and burned. And the healers told me that the dark figure was some kind of blockage, and that understanding the blockage was part of my reason for coming to them. In that moment, I knew I had to bring very specific intentions to my next ceremonies. I was going to focus on my feminine for one, masculine for the next, and intellect for the last.

For the second ceremony, I wore an ultra-feminine, draping robe in beautiful pinks and blues. That night, as the ceremony progressed, I lived the lifetimes of several female animals, from their birth to their giving birth and caring for their children. First, I was a grayish-white wolf with her pack and pups; then I lived the life of a female snake; then a female hawk, flying through the sky to her nest, feeding her chicks. Finally, I was a female black panther, loping through the jungle. And then I was gifted a crystal in the vision, a deep red stone edged in shining black, and an elder woman came to me and told me I was meant to give this stone to my masculine self, and that this would be the journey of my third night. All this time, through all these lifetimes, that dark figure was still standing to my right, and I couldn't see what it was or what it was trying to show or hide from me.

The next day, I told the healers about what I'd seen, and the medicine woman brought me in to look at her stones and crystals. She had one that was exactly like the one I'd seen in my vision the night before, and I took it with me to the ceremony that night. I dressed in an ultra-masculine, hard leather tank top situation, almost like I was going into battle. In my vision during the ceremony, I was this huge male gorilla, tearing through the forest and doing whatever he wanted—sleeping when he wanted to sleep, eating when he wanted to eat, fucking when he wanted to fuck, fighting when he wanted to fight. And then I was a soldier, or warrior, coming home to the woman he loved, still holding his battle ax covered in blood, and all he wanted at the end of the day was to eat with her, to be held by her, to allow himself a moment of vulnerability as he fell asleep in her arms. That's when I realized that the dark shape to my right, the one I couldn't look at, was my masculine self, and that I'd neglected it and had been letting it suffer. This part of me was wounded and needed protection. It needed healing.

In that moment, I understood that I'd turned away because I associated my masculine side with my father leaving when I was a kid, but even more so, with my uncle leaving when I was grown. I'd never been able to talk to him about it, never been able to mourn the loss. And it had just turned to poison inside me. I had also been turning away from my own cultural programming, as someone raised as male, not fully looking at all the ways patriarchal thought and misogyny had gotten inside me and affected my actions and relationships. And now I understood that I *had* to examine these parts of myself, not push them away. My life, my work, my relationships, my *love*—they all depended on it.

The night of the fourth and final ceremony, I suddenly realized that I could see. For the first time in my life, my left eye didn't feel lazy; the muscles of both eyes felt balanced, and I could look fully to the right. The dark figure was no longer obscured and I was no longer afraid to look. There he was, this giant fifteen-foot-tall man, finally uncloaked, his shadow getting smaller and smaller. That night, the deep sense came over me that the tears continuously leaking throughout my childhood that no operation could fix had actually been for a much greater purpose. I'd been accessing the grief of the universe, and that grief was pouring out of me. And it was in that moment that I realized tears can express any emotion, and that my tear-duct floodgates were always open, releasing the overflow of emotion, even after all the surgeries. The allergic shiners were a by-product of my lack of understanding this. I understood that I hadn't been taking care of my eyes, including my third eye, for most of my life, and that I had to keep them clear. They are the vessel that allows me direct connection not only with myself but with other people, and I'd been allowing them to work against me because of all the things I was unable to look at because I was afraid to *see*.

But after the final ceremony, I realized I was no longer afraid. My entire life was awash in the light of purpose. I was no longer afraid to die, and without that fear clouding my vision, I was ready to look at the parts of myself, and of the world, that had always terrified me. This sense of purpose, of meaning, was like a coal burning in my heart that started a blazing fire to incinerate my fear and illusions, and to make room for beauty and meaning and life to grow. I saw how much work I needed to do, how much I needed to dedicate myself to my true purpose of making this world into one where no body is the wrong body, one where we come to terms with history and start writing a new future for ourselves. Right here, right now.

I would have to teach myself, to learn all that I could, and I would need great teachers in order to become a teacher myself. We have to find the people who will help us let go of our old selves, the selves who are still scared of all the things they can't admit about themselves. Obviously a huge part of that understanding involved Bethany.

On the final night, right after I gave birth to myself as a white dragon (you can't even make this shit up), I saw Bethany and myself standing in an infinite forest. Quickly our bodies transformed into two massive trees, side by side. I could see that beneath the soil our roots intertwined for miles, straight to the core of the earth. Two individuals, connected forever. As our massive hardwood beings swayed in the wind, we became homes for multiple creatures—birds and mammals, reptiles and insects. We had the ability to provide them with shelter for any amount of time—maybe a few hours, maybe forever. And no matter what, our timber held strong.

And then there was Ian. Visions of who he was and what our potential could manifest as came flooding in throughout my whole week in the jungle. During one ceremony I saw him as the falcon flying in tandem with my dragon, two different entities entirely, yet able to take flight side by side. Even thousands of miles away, worlds apart, our bond was growing stronger.

One of the women doing the ceremonies hadn't been able to let go of herself, and I saw how much pain this caused her. How she struggled and struggled against the visions. I thought of my mother, my grandmother, my brother and his flame waiting to spark. The unconditional love we have for one another, constant and also troubled. I want them to be happy, to be free of the old pain. I want, through love, for them to be able to see.

It was time to go see my aunt and uncle. To close up the wound between us with the balm of love.


THERE WAS A monumental restorative balance that took place between my masculine and feminine energies while deep-diving through my subconscious with the help of a very powerful psychoactive medicine administered by the Shipibo healers. This type of healing work isn't readily available in the United States. Colonization erased many of the customs, rituals, and healing practices throughout the Americas—a loss that hurts all parties, including white people. Only by traveling to the Amazon jungle to experience a culture still rooted in ancient beliefs was I able to see how my own masculine and feminine energies directly correlate to my affiliation with my aunt and uncle. So the second I landed in Florida to spend Christmas at my mom's house, my mom, Bethany, and I got in the car and showed up on their doorstep. Well, at their fence. There was a giant fence with camouflage and barbed wire surrounding their entire property, barricading them in and keeping everyone and everything else out. We had called before we came, and they had agreed to the reunion. It was time to break through the wall.

As the gate screeched open, there they were. I couldn't actually believe it was them sitting in a heavy-duty golf cart, like the ghosts of my parents from another lifetime. In the blink of an eye I relived my entire childhood with them, and I started to feel so fucking grateful and even a little sad that most people would never be able to experience a reunion like this. I had already had a reunion of epic proportions with my father, but this was different—this was deeper. It felt like the next step in my evolutionary growth. Each step closer I took, I felt more impassioned and hot-blooded, and with each step, I shed another layer of trauma. All of us were already shaking and crying, my aunt probably more than anyone. Like my father, she'd apparently had a vision years before that this would happen. My mom was full-blown hyperventilating. She had always kept in close contact with her brother, talking to him almost daily (he'd basically raised my mom and they've always been best friends), even after he and my aunt left us abruptly and without warning. But they hadn't seen each other in almost a decade, and Bethany had only met them that one time, eons ago.

Bethany's demeanor was the most cautious—vigilant, even. They've always been the worst at hiding their real emotions, or rather, I can always see what's really going on behind their all-seeing eyes. It was almost as if they were my spirit protector, making sure I wasn't going to get hurt or disappointed again.

We hadn't really known the extent of my uncle's condition post-accident, yet there he was. The proud gorilla himself, turned a bit orange by the Florida sun, veneers whiter, hair lighter and longer, standing taller than I remembered. Yes, you read that right. Standing. Countless surgeries, physical therapy sessions, acupuncture, Reiki, raw food, and there he was. Up on his feet. Our not-so-peaceful warrior.

I had imagined this day a million times in my head. We toured the property and ate fruit from the trees, and my uncle prepared the most delicious raw vegan lunch. Sitting around the glass table on the lanai, we reminisced about the past and my uncle told jokes (he's fucking hysterical, and God, had I missed his laugh). We debated politics briefly, but I wasn't interested in arguing—that wasn't what I was there to do. Instead, I asked if we could play poker. "I thought you'd never ask," my uncle whispered as he pulled a rubber-banded wad of singles and a deck of cards out of his bag. Bethany returned to their usual bubbly pixie self and wound up winning the entire pot. And as my aunt brought out a spread of fruit for dessert and chlorella-infused coconut water, I was ready to confront my uncle.

During my time in the jungle, I had decided I needed to see him and had begun writing him a poem while I was there. I wasn't sure if I was going to leave it with him on the way out or audibly deliver the message, but as the day progressed, I knew what I needed to do. I had brought back a piece of pyrite (also known as fool's gold) on a necklace from the Shipibo tribe as a peace offering. That was the title of the piece I'd written for him: "Fool's Gold." I took maybe the deepest breath I've ever inhaled and began, fighting through every single emotion to get the words out:

*And so the day arrives. Student to master, towering over the man that once was. Arrival. No challenge but indeed questionnaire. Who is the man in the high castle crippled with fear? Who was the man on the mat that broke limbs for accolades? The man in the fur coat disco-ed. The bar owner, sobered. The one from Chicago that knew the streets in numbers. The foodie. The brother. The son. The husband. The guru. Your secrets echo through my veins. Obsessive. Compulsive. The lone gorilla. Stuck somewhere in physical body. Glued to chair. Once a warrior. Always a warrior. That spirit shifts but never disappears. The smartest man alive. Sage, oh sage, if it was true then still is. Leave me with one last journal entry and perhaps it will transcend finality. Fool's gold. Jack shit's flip side. Empty boxes. Filled.*

 *The boy once referred to as yours is filled. Brimmed. Years and years of resentment suddenly, miraculously, shift to gratitude. Appreciation. Perhaps this was the lesson all along. The disappearing act. The falsities. The training. Range Rover sessions, familial blessings. True abandonment. Sincerely much obliged. "Don't do stupid shits" mirror. From the pits of my heart, bulging muscles, smiling face, skin so tight my dick moves. You somehow continue to save my life.*

 *If you could do it all over again, would you shift intention? Alter tactic? Are you content in your selfishness? I* proclaim with confidence I wouldn't change a goddamn thing. The hole you left in my soul has been filled with so much love, light, positivity, and after all that's what cracks are for. Construction. Healing concrete. Because of your egocentrism I see now that selflessness and healing is sole purpose. Souls' purpose. A karmic path of devotion. Lone gorilla on his mountain top. I thank thee.

What will you be at the end of this? How is this making you feel? I encourage you to take this with utmost light. Olive branched. Fool's gold. When you think of me I hope you smile ear to ear. Your boy is indeed greater than you ever could have imagined. Superhumanly human. Worldly recognition. Saintly intention. Today humbled. A lover, an explorer, an artist. Always a student, universally. Every award, blessing, curse, challenge, in part a piece of you. Blood, sweat, chest hair, tears, brokenness, creationism. Action. Not quite what it looks like. Fool's gold.

Carlos Castaneda says, "The basic difference between an ordinary man and a warrior is that a warrior takes everything as a challenge, while an ordinary man takes everything as a blessing or a curse."

The challenge is this. Look past the fool's gold as I have. The stone's luster from afar superficial resemblance. Wealth. Abundance. Up close something else entirely. Iron sulfide. Pyrite. Fool's gold, though there is nothing foolish of said mineral. Hidden fire. Masculine in nature. Earth's energy. Protective. Sounds familiar.

Trees fall as do men. Crushing what isn't fast enough to move. Your king sago palm has been tumbling my way for

*more than a decade. Today I move. I hope you find it in*
*yourself to as well. Leap. Jump. Judo back flip. Get out of the*
*fucking way. This is the challenge. Not a blessing, not a curse.*
*A warrior's challenge. So much more than what it seems.*
*Fool's gold.*

Somehow I made it all the way through, barely able to take my eyes off the page, but when I did, he was staring directly into my soul while everyone else was in tears. Silence after the last words. I swear I could hear a hawk in the distance savoring his latest catch. And then my uncle uttered the only words I ever wanted to hear from him my entire life. Words that I had never heard before. An iteration of: "Wow. My boy. I have never been more proud of anyone for anything in my entire life."

And that was that.

The sun was setting, and we had a three-hour drive back to my mom's house, so we gathered our things and packed the car. When my uncle and I embraced on my way out, he told me that all the pain in his entire body had miraculously dissipated while listening to what I had to say. I stared into his eyes one last time, and without words I said: *Same. Same, girl, same.*

We've talked a few times since the reconciliation. There's never been a full explanation of the past, but no one is looking for one or trying to articulate it. We mutually understand the now is what matters, and that seems to be enough. We touch base on birthdays and if an issue in the family needs a more in-depth conversation, but it's mostly small talk. Not that long ago, I asked him what he was working on these days. What was he reading? What else was there to learn?

He responded with: "My boy, I'm done. There's nothing left for me to learn."

And then immediately I was reminded of the man who had helped raise me. The man who had had all the answers. The little kid in me wanted to kick and scream my way straight through the telephone just to prove a point. But the fact of the matter is, I don't know what it's like to be that age. I will never understand that feeling of complacency, no matter how much I seemingly accomplish. I may not be his boy anymore, as I don't even know what being a boy actually means. And no matter what, I love my aunt and uncle just the same, if not more, than I did growing up. Not as individuals, but as a unit. The masculine and feminine and the vast unspoken space between. Not in their relationship to each other and the world, but in their relationship with me and the human they shaped.

In so many ways my aunt and uncle are my original healers, my first teachers of plant medicine. By introducing me to the benefits of a raw food diet at a young age, they helped me form relationships with different plant spirits. I am a firm believer that every single plant holds a different energy, its own spirit entirely. And only through working with their medicines are we truly able to begin to understand the diversity of this incredible healing planet we inhabit. And no matter what, there is always something new to learn.

AFTER I RETURNED from seeing my aunt and uncle, and the trials and tribulations of Christmas with my mom, stepdad, and brother, Bethany and I flew back to New York. Ian met me at my apartment that night. We had already hooked up some before I left for Peru, but now things were different. I was different. Ian and I got in a car and drove upstate to spend New Year's Eve at an ashram. I'd just seen the universe during my trip to Peru, and the light of Ian came pouring directly in. My eyes were clear, and I was ready to see, to learn from this new teacher and to teach this new student.

The anniversary of my second year of sobriety was coming up, and it was dizzying how much I'd changed in such a short time. *The Love Bomb* would have never happened if I'd still been drinking. And in a lot of ways, the podcast documents part of my journey of healing, meaning, and integration. And that was part of what interested Ian. He had just recently made the decision to get sober from alcohol himself, and we really leaned on each other through it all. He could see that I was someone who was really trying to figure things out, and started pushing me to not only think bigger, but *deeper*, to peel back the layers of all the things I thought were true and understand the ways in which they were actually culturally and socially produced. Ian started filling up my bookshelves—with bell hooks, Leonard Cohen, Arthur Rimbaud, Maggie Nelson. I'd never read feminist, gender, queer anarchism, or critical race theory, and the ways in which these books showed me parts of the world I hadn't been conscious of before wasn't unlike the experience of taking ayahuasca. It was just a different kind of medicine, one that exposed harms and connections I hadn't even been aware of.

Ian really challenged me on race. We are both white, but Ian had done a lot of work to unpack what, exactly, being white means in this country, and he'd thought a lot about how being raised white had affected his experience, how he thinks, and what he cares about. Ian asked me if I'd noticed that every person I'd had on *The Love Bomb* up to that point was white. I had thought about it, yes, but at the time I didn't really have any friends or coworkers in New York who were people of color, and the last thing I wanted to do was actively seek out people to fill a token requirement. It needed to be a natural extension of my actual life. I had this moment of embarrassment, of feeling exposed, both because I hadn't figured out a way to make my platform more intersectional and representative of different kinds of people, and because I hadn't realized this was a huge blind spot that did a disservice to my mission. I didn't really have an answer for him, outside the fracturing ego spiral of white fragility. He gave me time to think about it, which is something he is good at: giving people all the silence they need.

Finally, I said, "I guess I've never seriously thought about it because I've never had to actively think about it."

"Right," Ian said in some iteration, "and you've got this podcast where you're only actually having conversations with particular kinds of people, for a particular audience, yet you're claiming it's universal. But you can't have something be about everyone, if 'everyone' turns out to only be white people."

It was so obvious, after Ian helped me see it, but it had been mostly invisible to me up until that conversation. My scope on intersectionality was somewhat limited up to that point. Sure, I knew more than the average person, but there was still so much further to go. Ian challenged everything I knew, or thought I knew. We got into heavy conversations on colonialism, the gentrification of New York City, how art and activism are racially influenced, and how important it was for me to broaden my understanding of the inner workings of our system. But as he was teaching me things, I was undoubtedly teaching him about the intersection of bisexuality, queer identity, and spirituality. How polyamory can exist in different forms regardless of any preconceived notions. The intersection of self-love and sobriety.

I started processing a lot of these thoughts and revelations through poetry. Writing has always been a way for me to articulate the space between how my brain operates and my mouth moves. My head was so full of ideas that poetry seemed like the best way to get everything out. Words just poured out of me. I was in the process of deconstructing all the things I thought were "real." I wanted to understand queerness and gender and fluidity, whiteness, class, and first-world privilege, to see how my gender, sexuality, and race had been built on top of one another. It felt like an important part of my spiritual development.

Meanwhile, as Trump was getting ready to take office, we were all seeing the different layers of ideology being revealed across the country. We were seeing the right and left, and just how far they'd moved away from each other, much more clearly, particularly on social media. It was almost like the two sides were speaking totally different languages. And it felt like the entire country was falling apart from wounds that have been here since the beginning.

A couple of weeks after our upstate trip, Ian invited me to

go to DC for Trump's inauguration to film an episode of *Gay-cation*. I had never been to DC before, and what better time to go than this. DC was a shitshow that week. The city was divided in two, a binary: half there to celebrate, half to revolt. And revolt we did. Different groups were protesting for different reasons, but things turned dark quickly. Smoke bombs going off, police in physical fights with the black bloc, cars getting turned over and lit on fire, people throwing shit from both sides. Full apocalypse. I would be lying if I said I wasn't a little terrified, but it exhilarated me. Seeing real protest in action, seeing how our rage is necessary, further changed my ideas about the kind of work I can do in the world and the best ways to approach it. Here were people from all over the country, maybe all over the world, showing up as bodies for cause in major ways. I knew I was ready to do the same.

After that, I started going to protests and keynotes and meetups in New York. Suddenly, my life became overtly political. Now everything I did, every choice I made, every reporter I spoke to, every photo shoot I went to, every piece of clothing I wore, every conversation I had, demanded political inquiry and motivation. My focus and goals were ever-changing, evolving through this new relationship with Ian and my response to the current state of the free world. We were this perfect pair. Yins to yangs, though it wasn't always easy. I had never dated someone as educated and articulate as him before.

Then, in February, I flew to Vancouver for a couple of months to shoot *Menendez: Blood Brothers*. I didn't ask Ian to come because I was playing the part of someone who killed his parents, and I knew that was definitely going to fuck me up.

Metaphorically speaking, there is something to be said about blowing your parents' heads off on camera. Maybe it mirrored the way I was detaching from my own programming.

When I got back to New York, my relationship with Ian was different. He resented the fact that I hadn't wanted him to come with me to Canada but realized I had been protecting us both. Ian had a way of telling me about the dark cosmos in his head in manners that were new to me. How we both had insecurities navigating the external projection. The majority of our relationship was the peace and steady *om* in which we found solace, but we had to decide how long it would last. Unsurprisingly, Bethany was a huge factor in it all.

In the early half of 2017, I was doing tons of cover stories and interviews in queer magazines like *FourTwoNine*, *alexa*, *Gay Times*, *JÓN*, and *PAPER*. The Page Six article from the previous summer had opened the door, and the podcast burst the floodgates. *The Love Bomb* was also getting tons of press, everything from *Vogue* to *Cosmo* to *The New York Times*. I was talking more and more about being queer in a public way, and I started to understand that part of being queer, for me, was about being vulnerable, about sharing with the world who I was actually *becoming*. The podcast gave people access to me, instead of me embodying someone else's character. I leaned into public vulnerability, no longer necessarily caring if I ruined my career, which my team still wondered whether I was sabotaging. Playing other people on camera is one thing, but playing myself in real life was exponentially more fulfilling.

In late spring, *The Advocate* called and asked if I wanted to do the cover story for their July 2017 issue. Holy shit, yes! And there's more. They wanted me to do it with Bethany, who had never been on the cover of a magazine before. This was huge. The story was called "This Is What a Queer Family Looks Like," and was about our very unorthodox relationship, which, at that point, had been going on for twelve years. Bethany and I hadn't slept together since Ian and I started dating. Bethany had a couple of not-so-serious relationships as well as a tumultuous off-and-on situation with one serious girlfriend, and I'd been in a same-sex monogamous relationship with a man for almost six months. *The Advocate* came to us because of my first podcast episode, in which Bethany and I talked about the different ways we've loved each other over the years, how we are family, no matter what form that took. This was also my second official coming out, two out of three. Bethany and I spoke at length about our interest in exploring polyamory and the challenges that come with facing socially expected monogamy.

There was a lot of backlash from that *Advocate* article because we came across as two white, cis, hetero-looking people claiming queerness. Queerness has been getting co-opted in the last few years by folks who don't really understand what it means—and let's be honest, myself included. So people were pissed, and Bethany and I understood why. From the outside, we look how we look, but our lives and realities are queer as shit. In a lot of ways, the backlash from that article led us to start figuring out how to articulate just who we were, both personally and in relationship to each other.

Around this time, our relationship started transitioning into something completely new, reborn. The *Advocate* article effectively demanded that we start talking about our future family in a very real way—should Bethany freeze their eggs, would I definitely be the father—and these conversations caused us to want to be physically closer again. We'd known for years that we were going to have kids together, we just hadn't talked about it since my ex-girlfriend and I split up. Bethany asked their girlfriend if she was willing to have an open relationship, and I asked the same of Ian. They both had to think about it, of course, and Bethany's girlfriend ultimately said yes. But weeks passed, and I couldn't really get a straight answer out of Ian, though he was willing to continue the conversation, and eventually was open to the idea. It was pretty much the first time Bethany and I had an open-relationship situation that was truly based in love, trust, and communication, rather than debauchery and experimentation.

The *Advocate* article was really confusing for Ian, and created a lot of questions. Which makes a lot of sense, considering that he was my boyfriend. The same weekend it hit the stands, we all were supposed to head upstate for the Fourth of July. Ian had asked me very normal questions about how the weekend would go and the logistics of our sleeping arrangements. I could sense he'd been anxious all day, and as it got later and later, his anxiety seemed to get worse. Finally, he asked which bedroom he would sleep in: mine, or the spare room? We couldn't see eye to eye—it seemed like we were having two completely different conversations—and this ultimately marked the end of our relationship.

Over the years, I've had the inkling that one is either open to a poly/non-monogamous relationship, or not. It feels like there's no middle ground. I know a statement like that seems to contradict part of the point of this book, but the space between does not exist without each end of the spectrum. Monogamy works for a lot of people, but through my own queer education, I understood that I wasn't one of those people. My final conversation with Ian was both memorializing and practical, commemorating our entire relationship inquisitively through ifs and hows and whys. I'm not sure we'd ever spoken to each other more frankly. Our time together was poetic and magical and deeply challenging all at the same time. I desperately wanted him to stay in my life as a best friend, but as I walked him to the train stop, I knew that wouldn't work. As we held each other on the street and kissed for the last time, the pain and pleasure of our entire relationship hit me like a brick.

Ian, I fucking miss you so much. This book would not exist without you.

IT'S FUNNY HOW much of a role the media played in bringing Bethany and me together in this new way that had also been there since the beginning. The universe delivered us to the world as a family on the cover of a magazine, and in many ways, that public representation gave us permission to move forward with our lives together in a way we hadn't been able to before. There was no map for us, so we became fearless in making our own way, doing things that felt right to us. We started talking a lot with each other about our respective relationships to gender, and Bethany was starting to articulate the ways in which they'd never felt like whatever a woman is supposed to be. I'd been getting much more in touch with my masculinity since Peru and seeing my uncle, and it's almost like the more I got in touch with it, the more I realized I wasn't really a man. *Not the wrong body, but the wrong world.*

As my political consciousness deepened, I began having serious doubts as to whether the best use of my celebrity was playing other people's characters in film and television. That was a kind of storytelling, sure, but I began to realize it wasn't the kind of storytelling that has the most healing potential. I'd been experimenting with different kinds of projects, both scripted and unscripted, different ways to use my platform for advocacy for queer and trans people, and how to make my own personal journey as useful as possible in the world. *The Love Bomb* was a huge part of this, of course, but I also wanted to put it down in words. Something that people could sit alone with and hold, contemplate, and then talk about with their friends. I wanted it in black-and-white print. And the result is this book.

That summer, I was invited to guest host *The View*. This was a monumental ask that came with a ton of responsibility. They wanted me to join an episode to talk about sexual fluidity. My first reaction was, *Yes, amazing! Here's a chance to have a real conversation regarding sexuality and gender identity on daytime television.* But the more I thought about it, the more I remembered my trip to Peru, and my conversations with Ian regarding accountability and intersectionality. I immediately realized I couldn't go on the show and talk about my experiences as a white, privileged member of society, as if I were the poster "boy" for fluidity. If they wanted me, they would have to include the work I was doing and the conversations I was having with people whose experiences were very different from my own.

Through *The Love Bomb*, I had really become a journalist in my own right, and this was my chance to show that gender and sexuality are always more meaningfully understood when that understanding takes into account the intersections of race, class, and privilege. I convinced the producers at ABC to help me rally a group of young adults with the help of the Lesbian, Gay, Bisexual & Transgender Community Center, which has been a queer haven and safe space in New York City since 1983. The executives at *The View* really wanted the show to focus on sexuality, but I very kindly explained that there's really no way to talk about sexual fluidity without touching on gender and other aspects of identity as well.

We gathered a group of six young adults who identify as something other than gay or straight, boy or girl, and I showed up at the center with Sara Haines, one of the show's cohosts, and a full television crew. I was able to facilitate a discussion with a diverse group of people, the majority of them queer youth of color who would not have normally been asked to speak on *The View*. Among the main topics we discussed was how being sexually fluid works in a relationship. In answer to Sara's question, "How much do you share right away?" one of the guests said, "I usually will just casually bring it up in conversation, like, 'Oh yeah, I had an ex-girlfriend, I had an ex-boyfriend.'" I was quick to agree. I said, "We're not usually dating people that don't understand who we are—at least, I'm not; it's not really an option for me."

This led into a conversation of how people are perceived and the energies we give off. One of the youth jumped in to explain the power of gaydar: "I think when you're queer, it almost becomes like a second nature to spot who is safe and who is not. When I walk down the street and I see other feminine people with shaved heads, we immediately make eye contact and I know exactly what is up with them. I got them, if anything happens, I'm right behind them."

And then we got into the question of why is it more socially acceptable for women to be bisexual. And we all ranted about the powers of the patriarchy and toxic masculinity, and almost in unison said, "Because women are fetishized . . ."

At the end of the segment, Sara turned to everyone in the room and asked, "So is anyone in the room attracted to me?"

Immediately I was reminded of the explicit reasons I had wanted to bring this conversation outside of myself. This segment actually wasn't about me, and it most definitely wasn't about Sara. And that is exactly why navigating this type of discourse with anyone who may not understand can lead to misunderstandings through false empathy. Why must we always revert to ourselves when talking about other people's identities and expressions? Okay, fine, it's human nature. But at what point, especially in the media and fields of journalism, are you really able to take yourself out of the narrative and actually listen to people who are different from you? And maybe you don't need to understand fully, but you can be respectful and appreciative. Everyone deserves equality, even the people you may not like. We all deserve liberation from repression, we all deserve safety and the ability to heal, and we all deserve the right to share our stories.

I know Sara was just trying to crack a joke and seem more relatable, and that she was there to genuinely try to understand. But in doing this, she ultimately made the entire conversation about her—it became about *her* ability to understand, or not, rather than about the experiences of the people who were speaking. Queer and trans people don't need cis straight people to *understand* us, but to accept that we have been here forever, and that their lack of understanding is the failure of a system that has consistently denied us our humanity.

And now the world is changing, and here we are, finally able to tell our stories in the mainstream. We all deserve a seat at the table. And although the experience with *The View* turned out to be a bit awkward and challenging, it is the one I am most proud of in my career thus far. This was solidarity. This was a step in the right direction.

## CHAPTER 9

THE YEAR WAS COMING TO AN END, AND WITH THE ANNUAL HOLI-
day calendar looming, Bethany and I got hit with a
major blow. The press surrounding our relationship was
too much for Bethany's family to process, and they disinvited
us to the Thanksgiving celebrations at their family's house. It
took weeks of conversations, emails, and family interventions
in order to get reinvited, and we went to their family's celebration from a place of love, refusing to allow the walls of oppression to box us in. But their family's momentary rejection of us
made us realize it was time to heal together, as a unit. We decided to go back to Peru, exactly one year after my first experience there. It was time to show Bethany what I had seen.

Two weeks before Bethany and I were scheduled to go to
Peru, I began working in earnest on my book of poetry. So
much had happened in the last year; there was so much just
waiting to pour out of me, and I let it pour. I mapped out the
entire book in one day, splitting it into three sections: body,

earth, and universe. A celebration of home. The home that is our body, the home that is this earth, the home that is our universe. Our existence in its entirety. So much of the work I had been focused on the year prior had been geared toward self-actualization through a broader understanding of the human condition. And when the opportunity to write a collection of poetry was gifted, I stared at the list of more than one hundred titles for poems laid out in front of me, and the title seemed to ascend within me: *all of it is you*. This was a theory of everything as simple as you—the first person to put the second person first, in everything. I had written half the poems by the time we left for the jungle.

I'd known the first moment I set foot in the jungle that I wanted Bethany to come back with me. We decided to go to a different ayahuasca center in the Amazon to create an entirely new experience together. Bethany had been in therapy for a couple of years by this point and was ready to take the next step in their own journey. I knew we were supposed to discover things about ourselves individually, and also together. I believed that the plant medicine would tell us something about how we were going to move forward.

But the divisiveness of gender was present, even in the jungle. Men and women weren't allowed to sleep in the same place, something I hadn't really noticed the previous year. Bethany and I weren't able to sit next to each other during the ceremonies because the healers and facilitators didn't want our energies too close while we were journeying. We were disappointed with the separation, but made our peace with it. We were guests in a sacred place, and we followed the rules as they were given to us.

The night of the first ceremony, I left my hut to walk about a mile in the dark to the *maloca*, the temple in the middle of the retreat compound where the ceremonies would be held. I was wearing a long, flowy, white silk *thobe* with a white pashmina wrapped around my head and had only a flashlight to light my way through the dense jungle darkness. The new moon was just rising and the night was pitch-black, the sounds of the jungle reverberating at high volume. At our orientation the first day we had gotten briefed on the wildlife in the area, and on my way to the *maloca*, I had a formal introduction to one of the greats. A red anaconda blocked my path. It was maybe ten feet long, as round as a basketball, easily able to crush a person of my size. I stopped dead in my tracks, full of primal fear, and realized that I was a trespasser in its home. I shined my light to the side of the path, in case the brightness was hurting its eyes. I knew I shouldn't run, that it would only startle the creature more.

I stood face-to-face with the reptile for at least ten minutes. I swear neither of us blinked once. Finally, I said out loud, "Please, great one, allow me to pass."

Dropping its head as if bowing, the snake slowly slithered uphill away from the *maloca*. And I booked it, running as fast as I could straight toward some sort of human contact.

When I finally arrived for the ceremony, hyped on copious amounts of adrenaline, all I wanted to do was burst through the wooden passage and tell everyone what I had just seen, but

I knew better than to bring that to them all before we jour-
neyed. The *maloca* was set up just the same as the one from the
year before. Mattresses lined the circular room, buckets were
set out for the purge, *palo santo* was burning, and the silence was
deep. We sat on mats in the pitch black, and one by one we were
called to the healer as he administered the ayahuasca. For the
first hour, there was just peaceful silence as we began our individual odysseys. And then someone started getting worked up,
becoming louder and louder with each breath until he began
screaming and wouldn't stop. "Jesus Christ, please protect me!
JESUS CHRIST, PLEASE PROTECT ME!" Harmless at first,
but it didn't stop.

I turned on my flashlight to see whose deep, accented,
masculine voice was disrupting the evening, and as the crimson hues lit his face, I was immediately terrified. The guy was
huge, over six foot three, with giant ropy muscles covered in
tattoos and a face full of rage. His forearms and hands were
like sledgehammers. One of the facilitators came around to
quiet him, but he kept screaming, this time summoning Archangel Michael, louder with each repetition: "ARCHANGEL
MICHAEL, PLEASE PROTECT ME!"

Most of the people in the ceremony had their eyes open
now and were watching him in the dim red lights. The giant
man got to his feet and stripped naked. He began punching
the wood walls, floors, and pillars of the *maloca* in an enraged
fit. It was horrifying. He kept screaming, and his blows were
so powerful that pieces of the wood began to splinter. We
had all taken ayahuasca, and the force of this violence went
straight to the depths of our beings. The healer and facilita-

tors rushed to him and I kicked into survival mode, immediately getting to my feet and running to Bethany. Meanwhile, he was getting more and more out of control, howling and jabbing at things at random, making contact with a few of the smaller female facilitators. Then he struck one of the male guests, and primal instinct kicked in: I screamed, "Everyone out!" We were shepherded out onto a balcony, while he was locked inside the *maloca* with the healer. Bethany collapsed in my arms, crying. "We're leaving. I got you, baby, I got you," I whispered into their ear. The terror was palpable; we had to get as far away from the *maloca* as possible. The facilitators escorted us to another structure half a mile north.

I had never felt more sheer horror in my life. We found a safe place on a balcony beneath the stars, away from whatever evil was present. Remember, we'd all just drank ayahuasca, and our journeys were officially just beginning. As traumatic as the experience had been, it wound up bringing the rest of us closer. I was terrified he would somehow escape the *maloca* and come for us. The collective journey up to this point was obviously not a pleasant one. As Bethany and I were curled up together on a mat, I looked up and saw a huge spider on the straw ceiling, reminiscent of the one from my journey the year prior. At that point, all the fear washed away—we had the insects protecting us. I know that sounds ridiculous, but at that moment, nothing felt truer.

We all settled in together, most of us in tears and fits, and continued our journeys, with the man raging in the distance. Time passed—I don't know how long—and then Bethany began to sob beside me. Just a little bit at first, and then their bawling began to ring through the jungle canopy. It was guttural, unlike any of the other sounds coming out of us. A sense of worry washed over the entire group; it was visceral. And then, amid the intense lamentation, Bethany said, "It's so beautiful," and the weep turned into a giggle. It was contagious. I started laughing hysterically, the rest of the group chiming in. The power of that laughter healed us all.

Bethany and I were holding each other, and their joy was healing to all of us. We were all having separate experiences, but that moment of trauma had knitted us very closely together. And there was the miracle of Bethany and me embracing during the ceremony, which wasn't supposed to have been possible, but which we both absolutely needed that first night. And the universe gave it to us. The medicine gave it to us. We all wound up passing out on the balcony, and when I woke up the next morning, holding on to Bethany harder than I ever had in my life, I said, "All of that happened so we could be together."

"I know," they said. "I know."

THE NEXT MORNING, we all came to breakfast, worried about what had happened to the man in the *maloca*, if he even survived the night. The head facilitator let us know he would be joining us for breakfast. I had never seen such a brute masculine force take over an entire space like that in my life, and now he was joining us for breakfast? What the fuck. As he stumbled through the swinging door, hands wrapped and bloody, head bruised and broken, face puffy, I saw that he was actually broken, beyond anything I had ever witnessed. He looked completely, utterly fragmented, like an embarrassed little boy. All his toxicity had turned to the vulnerability of tears, his tear ducts letting go of what his body was ready to release. He'd stepped through and touched the part of himself that he'd been afraid of, and it had caused him to crumble. He was naked before us, showing us his tears as an elixir, understanding how he had turned his fear to force, and how that had hurt people around him. I think most of the people there were still afraid of him, even in that state. But I saw that he needed to be touched, so I went to this large, muscular man and embraced him. I felt, very deeply, that he needed to have his vulnerability received by someone he saw as masculine, someone who was maybe like him. And I, too, crumbled in his arms.

I realized, almost immediately, that part of my work on this earth has to be focused on people who have been socialized as male and are trapped by the confinements of masculinity. My last immersion in the jungle gave birth to my current understandings of masculine and feminine energies, though there was still so much to be uncovered and deconstructed. We are taught as men, as humans, to hide who we are, to stray from our emotions; but one day, they will find an outlet, whether it be violence toward others, self-destructiveness, or both. Men need to help heal other men, especially in this social climate of identity politics. Up to that point, I was a man. But maybe that was about to change. If that's what a man is capable of, maybe I had the power to mutate both personally and socially. Maybe we all do.

I began to reflect on the intergenerational transference of trauma in my family, particularly in terms of gender. What was my uncle's relationship with his father like? What was my father's relationship with his father, and my stepfather's with his father, and on and on and on? And how and why had they replicated these relationships with me? In so many ways, the men in my family are still such a mystery to me. I have always been closer to women, having been raised primarily by women. My mom, grandma, and aunts trekked through for us, not for themselves. The men in my family, because of patriarchy, were unable to have that sort of protective awareness. We always see men as the ones who show up, the protectors. But so many men are unable to actually face their own demons. That is toxic masculinity. Men are so often not available to be held accountable or present as a product of being socialized to be "men." Part of my journey is also working to forgive them; even they were born into the wrong world.

The next six days were some of the hardest of my life, as I attempted to make sense of what had transpired. After our first ceremony, we still had an entire week ahead of us in the jungle. The man who'd freaked out wasn't allowed to drink ayahuasca again and, for the most part, was separated from us for the remainder of the week, working one on one with a therapist and healer. At the following two ceremonies I opted for super-low doses, because I wasn't ready to go all the way back in. I had seen too much, felt too much. So much deep internal healing came about for both me and Bethany, and for the entire group. We all left the center a family, tied together by traumatic yet healing experiences, exactly what a family is built on.

I want to take a second to give gratitude to the power of this plant medicine and the work surrounding it. The events that took place are unexplainable, for the most part, but I want to make sure this story doesn't scare anyone away from the opportunity to study. This was not a normal occurrence. That said, there's nothing normal about this type of work, and it should always be carefully considered and respected. It is not a fucking game. We all have a love and an evil that live inside of us, to some degree. And we all have the power to heal.

Our first night out of the jungle, Bethany and I made our way back to Iquitos, the land of the transient, and checked into an old hotel on the Amazon River. We hadn't had a shower or felt warm water in over a week, and after a much needed cleanse, we crawled into bed and slept and slept. The jungle had been exhausting, a hundred times harder than my first experience with the medicine. That's the thing about ayahuasca, or really life in general. You can't set expectations: life as such is capricious, revealing truths and falsities in its own time. But from this entire experience one thing became abundantly clear. In sleep I had a vision of Bethany and myself in white, flowing regalia, walking the streets of New York, seemingly from another time period. Numbers flashed in my frontal lobe: 399. 399. 399. March 9, 2018, 3/9/18 (in numerology the 18 becomes a 9). My eyes peeled open and I leaned over to the sleeping angel next to me.

"Baby, wake up. We're getting married on March ninth. I love you."

All they said was, "Okay, baby, I love you, too."

And just like that, we were engaged.

BACK IN NEW YORK, I took stock of everything and felt so much gratitude. My career seemed unstoppable, Bethany and I were getting married, and the poetry was just pouring out of me. The mantra coursed through my spirit—*all of it is you, all of it is you, all of it is you.* I finished the book two weeks after we got back from Peru. In forty-five days, I wrote a fucking book. We had rented a house in the Catskills for the winter, and life was seemingly perfect. And then my grandma called.

As far as I knew, she was still the only person in my family who didn't totally know about me. But at ninety-five years old, she was still running the antiques store, and one of her regulars thought it would be a great idea to show her a recent TMZ clip where I'm talking about queerness and polyamory. So, she called me right after seeing it. Bethany and I were driving through the mountains and I had my grandma on speakerphone. At first, she was pretending everything was cool, but I could tell something was up. I had been dreading this day since the second I knew I was queer.

After some small talk, she suddenly yelled, "NICO! You got anything to tell me?!"

"What the fuck are you talking about, you mean about getting married?"

"What are you talking about, getting married? I just saw

on TMZ that Bethany is a lesbian and you're a bisexual! What the fuck is a-matta with you?"

*Shit.*

The rest of that phone call was pretty violent. There was a lot of yelling and cursed silence. She hung up on me a few times, then called me right back, but that's a regular occurrence in my family. I attempted to explain myself to her using language I knew she would understand. It was right around this time that Bethany and I started deconstructing this idea of them coming out as lesbian and what that actually meant. I mean, we were getting married, we were sleeping together, so how would this actually read to people? I'm sure some of you have questions; we still do, too. And that is yet another extension of our fluidity. Language changes, as do people, and at certain times in our lives Bethany and I have both felt more comfortable using some words than others. And as our understanding of gender and sex continues to evolve, so does our basis of sexuality. I tried explaining all that to my grandma, but there comes a certain point when communicating with folks from that generation—and her in particular, given her upbringing—where nothing you say actually matters. My words were obscured by her past and by history's oppressive nature. She cut me off for a while, refusing any sort of communication for months. She can really be a fucking asshole, but you know what? I. Still. Love. Her. No. Matter. What.

NOT LONG AFTER THAT, I got a message on Instagram from someone I had been introduced to on the internet, Alok Vaid-

Menon. Aesthetically, Alok was unlike anyone I had ever seen: unapologetically flamboyant in their gender nonconformity, with fashion looks to match. Flagrant displays of femininity through their somewhat traditional masculine physical traits. Your favorite girl-boy in color, always in color. They asked me for my address so they could send me their latest book of poetry, *Femme in Public*. When the book arrived in the mail, a handwritten note inside read: *Nico, the world is shit. You make it better. Looking forward to building something else together. Love, Alok xx.*

Their mind-boggling looks, intellect, and activism were absolutely amazing, but their words completely blew my mind. We didn't know each other in the slightest, yet that simple introductory greeting spoke volumes. They had a vision—one of me, one of them, one of us together—and visions of this world that I had never even considered. And if you've learned anything about me up to this point, it's that I respect a vision.

As a Texas-raised Indian American gender-nonconforming trans feminine performance artist who uses *they/them* pronouns, their activism was special. Not only were their bodies of work centered on the collapsing of conservative binaries and divisions, but they also focused on the problematic structure of progressive movements. A true artist challenging and analyzing every system built to destroy us. Art allows us to say the things we wouldn't normally be able to articulate in our waking life, and Alok has a lot to say. The book was unlike anything I'd ever read; it was breaking down race and gender unapologetically from a place of pain and empathy. The cover is an image of Alok in a formfitting little black dress with their arms up behind their head as a sort of protected invitation, with a look on their face of sexiness, vulnerability, and intimidation all in one. Body hair protruding from every area of exposed skin. Makeup and jewelry in addition to the bindi stamped in the middle of their forehead, all with the perfect amount of five-o'clock shadow. The first line of the book reads, in all caps, "WHAT FEMININE PART OF YOURSELF DID YOU HAVE TO DESTROY IN ORDER TO SURVIVE IN THIS WORLD? I'M TRYING TO FIGURE IT OUT."

They then continue with questions that hit my core:

*what would it look like to leave the house and not be afraid of getting bashed? what would it mean to leave the house and not be bashed? what would it mean to leave the house and not be harassed? what would it mean to leave the house and not be objectified? what would it mean to leave the house and not be gendered? what would it mean to no longer be forced to do the work of gender? what would it mean to have a self beyond my body? what would it mean to log online and not being told to die? what would it mean to have people say "i'm here" instead of "you're fabulous"? what would it mean to no longer have to be fabulous to survive? what would it mean to be able to go home wearing what I want? what would it mean to be desired for me and not my body? what would it mean to be desired for me and not my body?*

*    is it that i don't remember anymore or that i never knew?*

My poetry had bits and pieces of this type of theoretical inquiry, but most of *all of it is you.* centers around the idea of oneness—a universal understanding of the divine frequency of love that unites us all. But what Alok's work did was force me to see beyond my body and privilege. This is someone who gets harassed and spit on when they walk outside in a dress, and then writes about it, chants it through the ether on social media as a form of cathartic healing for themselves and for anyone who chooses to listen. I didn't have a choice but to listen. Like a brand-new sponge fresh out of the cellophane, I wanted to take it all in. A new type of relationship I never knew I needed.

I devoured the book over and over again. With every page, every word, every self-portrait and photograph, a new guttural emotion was unveiled. Who was this person? Where did they come from? And what was in store for our future? Prophetically, they already saw something, but what, exactly, was yet to be determined.

I sent Alok a copy of my poetry manuscript, which was set to be published two months later, and we arranged to meet in a café near Union Square. I walked in, elated to finally meet Alok in person. As I sauntered through the lingering fragrance of incense and vegan food, I spotted Alok at the window table, in a classic bombastic ensemble. Layers of colorful leggings underneath a floral-printed skirt with yellow patent leather pump boots. Given our texts and email exchanges, I'd expected Alok to greet me with a big hug, for us to be instant best friends. But Alok was somewhat aloof and very serious, almost like none of our correspondence had ever happened, as if there were a wall protecting them from any sort of impending threat I could bring. The interrogation began. We discussed the binaries, transness, community, poetry, race, class, Hollywood, art, relationships, love, marriage, Bethany, family, spirituality, and so forth—brick by brick, dismantling every topic. Hours passed in minutes. And finally, as if waiting to tell me the entire time:

"I didn't expect to like you because you're a white Hollywood star," they said. "Honestly, I thought you might be doing this for the attention."

Body slam. I had been critiqued over and over again by strangers on the internet, and even by the people closest to me, Ian included, but Alok gave me the opportunity to show myself to them first, in person, the real me, before deciding if I was worthy of their friendship. I had apparently passed the test, and it was one I was more than willing to take. From the bottom of my heart, the exploration has always been genuine. I have always wanted to feel more, know more, help more, and Alok demanded that I listen to that instinctual force.

I'd never met anyone like Alok before. They weren't just critiquing conservatives, but also progressives, and the ways in which even leftist thought and policy have within them old racist, classist, sexist, queerphobic, and transphobic ideologies. Shortly after our first encounter, Alok started listening to my podcast and reading my poetry. They started breaking down my shit with queer theoretical commentary in both an academic and emotional way. Alok challenged me to realize that the work I was doing with *all of it is you.* was, in fact, centered in the collapsing of binaries and divisions. I had always known this, but Alok expanded the way in which I understood that work and its intentions.

A couple of weeks after I met Alok, Bethany and I went to see their show. Alok is the definition of performance art, and they had made it very clear when I first met them that everything would make so much more sense when I saw them in their true element. They had a show in a basement near Soho with one of their best friends, the nonbinary trans feminine poet and activist Travis Alabanza. Travis hit the stage first with an aggressively sensitive spoken-word performance that centered around their gender and being, and I was immediately transported to another universe entirely. And then Alok stepped up, in a floor-length pink faux-fur robe with a train, and the minute they began to spit into the microphone, my world was flipped upside down. I could not stop crying, every verse crawling deeper into my gut. I'd never heard someone talk so passionately about the harassment of trans and gender-nonconforming people in art, all while jumping back and forth from comedy to pain to love.

Alok seemed to direct their performance to me, and started making fun of Hollywood and systemic racism and how it was up to us to start changing the narrative. They talked about how we need to actually show up, in a real, material way, for trans feminine people of color, instead of just posting photos for street cred. Then they came for Bethany, dismantling body image through the lens of basic white-woman feminism, and for the first time I realized that femininity and its movements can be toxic, too. I'd seen it firsthand in my mom and my grandma and every other woman who helped raise me, how the ways in which they asserted power over a situation could be just as dangerous as a man exercising power. I'd seen it in the ways in which certain white feminist movements claim originality and inventiveness and forcefully disregard women of color, trans women, and nonbinary folk. They fail to see that just because you're getting strangled doesn't mean your hands aren't wrapped around someone else's neck as you gasp for air.

Alok has a way of forcing the audience to be engaged, quipping with the perfect balance of art, humor, and trauma. They insist that everyone in the room look inward and challenge every single part of themselves. A sort of self-awareness and societal awareness that took us all to church. As the sermon came to a conclusion, I felt as if I had finally seen the truth. I'd been introduced to the nucleus of everything I had been fighting for since I had gotten sober. I hadn't even known what that actually was until I met Alok. To truly understand oppression, you have to understand yourself as an oppressor. I wanted to do anything I could to know more, feel more, do more.

I left the show a complete wreck. Never in my life have I cried more, or felt more, during any sort of show I'd ever seen, *Rent* on Broadway in 1999 included. I took what I learned from Alok, the insidiousness of my own privilege, and started coming to terms with my own gender identity. I had known gender-nonconforming and nonbinary people prior to Alok, but until I met them, I had never felt I was deserving of such titles because of my primarily masculine physical expression. I don't look like what people may consider gender-fluid, so for the longest time I insisted I was cis. But Alok helped me realize that I'd had it in me all along. *Not this, not that, beyond definition* was more than just a mantra carved into my chest. It was my core. *All of it is you, all of it is you, all of it is you.*

Gender nonconformity is just that—nonconforming. I didn't have to look fringe or feminine on a daily basis to be nonbinary. Gender is what exists on the inside and inspires who we are on the outside. But the two are not always in tandem. And through my own understandings, Bethany began to comprehend just how wide the chasm really is. Alok challenged the fuck out of Bethany, taking them to task over what it means to be a woman, what it means to have a vagina; how the conversations around femininity can also be misogynistic, imperialist, and transphobic; the disconnect between genitalia, gender, and autonomy. Not all women have vaginas, not all men have penises. In a lot of ways, Bethany and I represented enemies in the community for Alok and for so many other people. We still do. As white, cis-passing, straight-passing folks having these conversations on platforms that don't normally adhere to gender or queer politics, we could help each other with messaging. And the platonic love affair with Alok commenced.

BETHANY AND I knew we wanted to be married in the Office of the City Clerk at 141 Worth Street in Lower Manhattan, and we knew we wanted it to be just us. No one else was invited. The downtown courthouse exists solely for marriage purposes, and let me tell you, this place is special. The way it works is quite simple. You first have to go there at least twenty-four hours and no more than sixty days before your wedding to obtain a marriage license. This allows them to filter out any inebriated last-minute decisions to get hitched. Immediately when you enter, the rush of love is almost blinding. From the street vendor outside selling rings and flowers to the couples and families from all walks of life, their outfits representing all parts of the world, to the smiling faces of the employees, security guards, police officers, all of whom are strangers, all welcoming the holiest of matrimonies.

The night before, our dear friend Andrew Morrison, who designed our gender-bending wedding ensembles, had come over for a last fitting. These looks were everything we'd ever dreamed of. Timeless androgynous garb mimicking marble Romanesque sculpture, fluidly blending our masculine and feminine. In this relationship, we both wear the pants and the dress. And we topped each other off with crowns. Yes, we wore crowns—it felt like something we'd done in a past life, so we had to keep the tradition alive. In this life's iteration, this was, in fact, our royal wedding. We gathered up everything we would need for the day, called a car, called on spirit, and headed outside to do the damn thing.

We got to the courthouse a little later than expected, but since we had decided to ride solo for this adventure, no one cared. We were immediately welcomed by smiling faces. Unspeakable pride rushed through my entire being. We posed for a few pictures and made small talk with the other lovers getting married and their families, and I was already so emotional that I started crying. While we were waiting in the corridor just outside the East Chapel, a man's voice echoed through the alabaster chambers—*"Nicolo and Bethany."* This was actually the first time I'd heard my full first name spoken out loud by a stranger. It was time.

The person who married us was named Angel, but he was not the only angel present. All day long it looked as if angels were present, far and wide. Our ceremony lasted less than two minutes.

Do you, Nico? I do.

Do you, Bethany? I do.

And from the mouth of an angel, it was official: "You may now kiss the bride." We opted for no rings and had a plan to exchange our own vows after the courthouse. In hindsight I wish we had asked Angel to use nonspecific gender titles, but so be it—this husband now had a wife, and this wife now had a husband. Or, to be more precise, we now both had, and were, a wife and a husband.

There were congratulations and cheers all around from passersby as we left 141 Worth Street. As we sauntered through the Financial District, where Greek Revival architecture is ubiquitous and thus created the perfect backdrop for our neo-Grecian drape dress, time seemingly stopped altogether. We had a proper photo shoot, sans proper permits, but this was our wedding day. We were going to shoot bull's-eyes, no matter what.

We hopped in a cab to our next destination. I'd decided the night before that I wanted to head to a church to read our vows to each other. The oldest church in Manhattan, St. Paul's Chapel, was just the spot. People spend years planning a wedding and reserving churches, and here we were just winging it, as angels do. After passing through metal detectors, we doused ourselves in holy water, said a prayer, and approached the altar. Now, there were plenty of people in this church, but I swear to God we were the only two people in one of the oldest, holiest places in all of New York City.

There we were, two kids from the Midwest who fell in love almost twelve years ago on the South Side of Chicago. We grew up together, we grew up apart. We taught each other how to love. We've pushed social constructs and broken boundaries. We've confused our friends, families, lovers, coworkers, the media, and even each other. We've said and done the right things and most certainly the wrong things. We've been boyfriend and girlfriend, boyfriend and boyfriend, girlfriend and girlfriend, no friends, and all friends. We've been sober, addicted, straight, confused, queer, bi, lesbian, poly, and gender enthusiasts. We've been lovers—*are* lovers—twin flames. And we will be *forever*. Hopefully a piece of love has jumped from these words to you. This is our now, shared with you, and tomorrow is a future for all of us.

THAT MAY, I had the incredible honor of hosting an event for the GLAAD Rising Stars Grant Program, which celebrates young people's commitment to accelerating LGBTQ acceptance within their communities and the culture at large. Grants are offered to support young people who are leveraging media to move hearts and minds and create change. It was such a profoundly moving and emotional experience. And if there was ever a time to make bold fashion choices, it was now. But this was about way more than wearing a dress—this was political. It was no secret that my sexuality had been ever evolving, and quite recently my own gender identity had been taking on a new expression.

My friend Christian Siriano dressed me in this asymmetrical electric-green zebra-print suit jacket and skirt. In my opening monologue, I said, "Hey. Guess what? We made it to earth! We have no idea why we're really here, but we have bodies, we have minds, we have spirits. We have laughter and rainbows, every color of the spectrum. We have community, we have our elders that paved the way, we have our youth who are rewriting what it means to be queer, and we have each other. Now, we all know that we're living in some trying times, y'all, but listen. Without the bad, the glad doesn't exist. Without the bad, GLAAD doesn't exist. I encourage everyone in this room to always lead with love, no matter what."

The following night I wore a strapless black-and-white billowy-sleeved cocktail gown to the GLAAD Awards and Bethany wore a classic masculine suit. Gender fuckery. I was the first gender-nonconforming human ever to wear one of Christian's gowns on a red carpet, but for sure I won't be the last. I wore it to honor young trans and gender-nonconforming folks in the hopes of giving them another positive representation of themselves. And also because I looked fierce as shit. But I would be lying if I said I wasn't blindsided when my mom FaceTimed me the next day. She'd probably played the game of telephone with her sister, my uncle, and Rocco to work herself up properly before picking up the phone. I knew she was coming to fight. And the punches started flying.

"I can deal with your sexuality, but why must you always take it to the next level? I've come such a long way, but this is too much for me." Somehow, she always makes shit about her. But I held my ground and stayed patient . . . until she said, "Just fucking tell me, are you Caitlyn Jenner now?!" The queen in me gasped, then laughed out loud before replying, "I meannnnn . . . I'm not *not*!!!" (*All of it is you* . . .) Then my masculine brawn kicked in—"ARE YOU KIDDING ME?!" I went off, Tyson-style, and metaphorically gnawed off her ear straight through that telephone.

"Mom . . . I am not transitioning, at least not in the way you fucking think I am. We are ALL ALWAYS transitioning in some way, though, Mother!"

"Oh, here we go, Nico." My mom knew I was ready for this.

I went on to explain, "Nor do I feel I am in the wrong body. My transness, my gender nonconformity is not like anyone else's—it is mine. For so long I felt I was unworthy of a nonbinary label because of what I looked like and what society expected of me."

Silence. A long pause. My mom is never silent. *This must mean progress* . . .

"Just tell me why, Nico. Why a dress?"

"Mom. I do not wear a dress because I feel more comfortable. In fact, that dress was insanely uncomfortable. I wear the dress as a form of protest. This is beyond my gender identity, this is political. I wear this dress because I can. Because of my platform, my celebrity, and what I look like, I am celebrated in the press the next day while my friends are spit on and yelled at for wearing dresses on the street. I wear this dress to disrupt the system. I wear the dress for every kid out there who ever felt like their femme didn't belong. For every kid who was contemplating suicide because they didn't see a version of themselves in the mainstream media. I wear this dress for myself second and *everyone else* first. For everyone who screams, 'YES, BITCH!' and for everyone who screams, 'DIE, FAGGOT.' And Mom, if you, my best friend in the whole world, still don't understand that, after the hours of queer conversation we've had, and after all the success I have already had?! There is obviously still SO MUCH MORE WORK TO BE DONE!"

After a long pause—my mom wasn't sure how to respond—Bethany entered the room and told us that their mom had been in the hospital for three days with a lung mass. My mom and I immediately dropped our guards and showed up for Bethany, asking them questions to help them figure out next steps. As soon as they left the room to put their plan for their mom into action, I turned back to my phone.

I took a breath and asked, "So, what do you want for the rest of our relationship, Mom? When you never know how much time you have left, what do you want from the rest of our relationship moving forward?"

There was another pause. I sat looking down, with my hands holding each side of my face. Then she answered.

"As it is. Which is that we talk to each other in the morning and text each other at night. I always know that you're there and you always know that I'm here. That's important. The reality of life is that families separate and hopefully see each other once a year, but as long as we stay connected . . . I mean, if it wasn't for FaceTime, this would be horrible. I feel connected to everything that you do on a daily basis, even if I don't understand it, because you allow me to be connected. I couldn't ask for anything more than that. . . . Unless I buy that house next to you and move in, then I'll be a major pain in your ass."

My mom, always with the one-liners, the funniest fucking person I've ever met. And as her son, who just wants their mom to be proud, I asked: "What would you say you are most proud of? In terms of what I'm doing with my life."

"I guess I would say I am proud of all of you," she said. "I see you. I am beginning to understand how you are helping people and changing people's lives by nothing I understand, but they understand it. And the impact you're having on complete strangers. The difference you're making. Not just for me on a daily basis, but seeing how complete strangers have reached out to you and say that you've changed everything for them. That's pretty special."

"All of it is you, Mommy," I said, as I blew her a kiss. "I love you."

"Thank you for always taking the time for me, for explaining. I love you, too, baby."

We never say good-bye. We always end our conversations with *I love you*.


WHEN I POSTED the pictures of me at the GLAAD Awards on Instagram, I basically came out to the world as nonbinary. And it was after the conversation with my mother that I started playing with using *they/them* pronouns for myself and for anyone I can, when it's appropriate. We are *all* multidimensional dynamic creatures, and as much as I understand the spectrum, the less I believed in the binary of gender, and the more liberated I was becoming. Facial hair, body hair, blue steel, leg pop, hip pop, and all. I was alive, I was free, all of it was me.

Without Alok, I don't know if this ever would have happened. They pushed me way out of my comfort zone, and I experienced the third coming out of my trinity. First I was fluid, then I was poly, and now I am nonbinary. Needless to say, people had some fucking opinions.

My professional team and I started really getting into it. I sent out an email saying I would prefer everyone internally to start using *they/them* pronouns when referring to me directly and indirectly. It didn't go over as planned. Everyone had something to say that somehow had nothing to do with me, but with their own inabilities to see past the binary. I sat on a call for over an hour with my publicist and agents, pleading and spitting theory. If I couldn't get them to understand who I was, how could I get anyone else to? By the end of the call, everyone agreed to give it a try, but it hasn't been going over as well as I'd hoped. Every single day is a work in progress, a transition. I'm still juggling the challenges of identifying as nonbinary, working in an industry that is built on the binary. Some days are better than others, and some people make the effort to use the correct pronouns, but most of the time I have to deal with the fact that most people are not even willing to try. I know in my heart of hearts that *they/them* pronouns best portray who I am, internally and externally. But if *all of it is you*, I'm able to find truth and reason in all pronouns.

ANOTHER THING I have Alok to thank for is my coming to embrace my own potential as a performer. My book *all of it is you.* officially dropped on April 17, 2018, and touring with it gave me the perfect opportunity to spread my wings. After seeing what Alok had been able to inspire through performative art and spoken word, I started curating a live set for the book release party. I bought a fancy voice modulator, the same one Alok uses, and began to play with sounds in a way I never had. I bought a set of tuning forks, instruments used to heal through vibrations, and started creating a sound bath to underlie the poetry. I became obsessed, crafting full two-hour sets. I reached out to one of my best friends from high school, a musician, to work together on producing tracks I could use for the live show. The night of the book launch, I performed for two hours on Instagram live. A full set of spoken word, experimental sound, and vibrational healing. I asked Alok if they would join me on stage mid-set. If people were coming to see me, the white "dude" from television, I wanted to introduce them to the person who had inspired so much of my work and personal development.

In one way or another—and I know this is going to sound like a reach—I found God in performing this book. Alok talks about performance art as therapy, something I was beginning to understand. Now, it certainly isn't for everyone, but the people who understand what it was I was attempting to do wound up flocking to these events. I was expanding my community internationally through performance art. I open each show with the idea of collapsing binaries and divisions, including the split between performer and audience. I bring people from the audience onstage and let them use the platform in any way they see fit. People spill their hearts to complete strangers. I've created self-love-based group therapy, and its potential is only just beginning to come to fruition. Going on tour made me even more of a spokesperson around the country and around the world.

That summer, I did a two-show weekend in Chicago and my entire family came. My mom and brother had already been drinking by the time they got there. And my loud-ass family talked all the way through the show. Within two minutes of the show starting, Rocco came up onstage, busted out with an interpretive dance, and then went into full lotus position five feet away from me. I thought for a second about how the old me would have been so pissed—my bro trying to steal the limelight—but I shared the space with him. He's my brother, I love him.

But we'd had a tumultuous relationship since I'd gotten sober. I knew it was hard for him to see me being so out, so political, so myself. We'd never had a conversation about me becoming a spokesperson. In fact, there were a lot of things we could no longer talk about since I'd gotten sober. As a person who's sober from alcohol, it's hard to be around anyone drinking as it is, but to see my brother, my twin mirror, staring back at me with the same pain struck deep.

So when Rocco did his interpretive dance while I was trying to perform, that was cool with me. He's always supposedly been growing up in my shadow, remember, the kid who would set the world on fire if he could just strike the match. Except that his matchbook got wet.

But I believe the sun is out. The sun is out, and soon my brother is going to light his blaze. To my sorcerer brother who loves deeper than any other: *What would you do if a dolphin crashed through the ceiling?* You say a prayer, jump on her back, matchbook in hand, ride her through the city streets lighting up every face you see, and show the world you're ready to attack, gracefully. And never forget, Rocco, *the sun is out.*

IN EARLY JUNE, I was asked to participate on a panel called "Breaking Down the Binary" at the ATX Television Festival in Austin. The panel consisted of Cameron Esposito and Rhea Butcher (*Take My Wife*), Aisha Dee (*The Bold Type*), and me. The panel was set up to be a celebratory and informative discussion about representation and inclusion in the industry. Everything was going great, until this guy dressed in a computer costume—you can't make this shit up—stood up and started heckling us, saying nonbinary wasn't real and all this other homophobic, transphobic, conservative bullshit, all in a computer voice. Fucking idiot. We all talked to the guy, to get him to stop interrupting the panel, and then all of a sudden he rushed the stage. He was screaming, throwing out *fags* and *dykes*, and my own toxic masculinity kicked in. I got up in his face, screaming back, ready to beat the shit out of him. And then it occurred to me that the guy was obviously unhinged, and that he might have a gun. We were in Texas, after all. I'd never been attacked in any way for being queer before, and though I was angry, I was also terrified. Eventually, a security guard dragged the guy out. As he was leaving, I came back to my senses and screamed, "I love you, I love you, I love you" to him. Other people weren't happy with my quickness to forgive. But this person was obviously in pain, and I started to feel bad for him.

After the panel was over, I was still upset, and the first person I called was Alok. As comical and ridiculous as the experience had been, it was also really unsettling. Alok had been on that end of harassment, and I relived the entire experience for them. They reminded me more and more about the grief all of us are carrying around, in different ways, and how even the people who don't accept us—the ones who hate anything deemed different—are hurting inside. And they take out that hurt on people they see as "other." As my own mantra rolled off their tongue, *all of it is you, all of it is you, all of it is you*, I was moved to tears.

Having something shitty like that happen only made me want to do more. I'd had a tiny glimpse of what some queer and gender-nonconforming people face every day, and I was more certain than ever that the course of my work would be changing this world we live in. Oppression hurts oppressors, too, and taking this into consideration is a large part of healing.

After the ATX panel, I began speaking out more about

trans deaths and violence. In July, I was invited to give the keynote speech at the Her Conference. And the first emotion that ran through me was confusion. Why me? I am not a traditional "her." I mean, my queer friends use *she/her* pronouns as terms of endearment, but I don't think that's the same. I found myself spiraling about my own gender and queer identity, thinking about what it would feel like to be someone who looks like me up there talking to a group of women. I immediately texted my regulars.

First up, Bethany. They immediately threw up their feminist defense mechanisms. "How dare the Her Conference invite you to speak, let alone keynote." This was the thought that had already been running through my own head. I said, "Baby, I hear you."

"You are not a her," Bethany said. "You are taking a seat at the table away from a woman. In this political and social climate, in the trenches of the #MeToo movement, we need to take into consideration how important it is for women to be able to speak without men speaking for them."

"I hear you loud and clear. I want to remind you that I am not a man. And this could be an opportunity to expand on that in a space where it's important."

Bethany paused, then said, "Ugh, text Alok and call me back."

Alok responded with: YES, YOU SHOULD DO THIS. THEY WILL GAG. SO IMPORTANT TO OCCUPY THESE CIS WOMEN SPACES.

I called Bethany back straightaway and relayed Alok's blessing. We both have learned so much from Alok in such a short amount of time. But I needed Bethany's blessing as well to justify my involvement.

"Baby, it is so, so, so important for me to use the opportunity to shine light on the violence the community is facing. No one else that is speaking at the Her Conference will be. Please. Can you understand that?"

I could hear the layers of their own oppressions being unmasked, the layers of historical binary buffoonery falling away, as they replied, "Why does this all have to be so confusing? Break a leg, baby. I love you."

"I love you, too."

Later when I practiced my speech for Bethany, they fully understood the weight and importance. They couldn't have been more proud and supportive. Sometimes it just takes a little time to get there, but doesn't everything that really matters?

A FEW WEEKS LATER, I spoke from a podium at the Her Conference to hundreds of cis women for over an hour. They asked me what song I wanted playing as I entered the space like I was about to enter a match. I opted for Whitney Houston's "I'm Every Woman" to really set the tone. *It's all in me.* All of it is you. *All of it is you all of it is you all of it is you* softly hummed through my consciousness throughout the entire speech. And as the speech was coming to a close, I really dug my heels in and had a few final things to say:

Queer and trans people, and especially people of color, are being bashed and murdered at higher rates than ever before. Most of the times when trans or nonbinary people are killed, they are mis-gendered and never properly recorded. When Matthew Shepard, a white cis gay man, was killed, the entire country banded together. And that's just here in the United States. Overseas the number of transfeminine folk that are killed every year is uncountable. Unimaginable.

These numbers do not include the suicides.

These numbers do not include the bashings.

These numbers do not include the verbal abuse.

These numbers do not include the domestic violence.

These numbers do not include the catcalling.

These numbers do not include economic violence.

These numbers do not include the rights being stripped away by the current administration.

These numbers do not include sexual health and reproductive violence that is being committed by this administration.

These numbers do not include the violence cis women propel on trans folk every single day by simply excluding them from these conversations.

Queer rights, and trans rights, are inherently women's rights. "Hers" rights. FEMININE RIGHTS. The more we feed into the binary, the more divided we become. Thousands of years ago, the feminine reigned supreme. However, the feminine spirit is rising again. We are here. But now the question remains: How do we listen to the feminine spirit and not reproduce the gender binary? How do we listen to the feminine spirit and not neglect trans and gender-nonconforming people?

I say all this as a reminder. What is feminine is not defined by what is or isn't between your legs.

I repeat. Despite what trans exclusionary feminists passing anti-trans legislation across the world and halting Pride marches have to say, what is deemed feminine is NOT defined by what is or isn't between your legs.

Our system is broken, yes. Misogyny is real, yes. The patriarchy is real, yes. The female struggle has been more real than the male struggle for eons, yes! But the sooner we all band together—women, men, and everyone in between—to not fight this issue but to correct the imbalance, the sooner we will have some love-based social order in this world.

All of it is you.

Be every human. Love every human. See every human. Respect every human. My call to action is this: as much as we are aware of the victim in all of us, we must also acknowledge the ways we are complicit. Just because you are being strangled doesn't mean your hands aren't wrapped around someone else's neck. If you see something, say something. If you have a body that is deemed more socially acceptable than others, stand up for the ones in need. If you are white, scream against systemic racism. If you are an American citizen, stand up for undocumented people. Stand up for the indigenous, the poor, the Black, the trans, the you, the me, the us.

We were all born here. Equal spirits divided into unequal bodies.

Include all.

Love all. Because all of it is worth celebrating.

Because all of it.

Is you.

S O, THAT'S MY STORY, UP TILL NOW. I'M BACK UPSTATE, IN THE house where I first started this writing journey. My God, Gods, angels, and spirits are all still here. Maybe even a few more have joined us, and I'm looking at my altar, with all the herbs, images, and ritual objects I've collected over the years. I've just purified myself, the house, and my computer with *palo santo*, and through the large windows I can see it is a gray, cold January day. The trees are bare, the waters of the marsh are frozen over, and the geese have migrated. Last night, there was a full-moon lunar eclipse; I watched alone with a fire blazing in the hearth as I burned the index cards that had adorned my walls as an offering. It was a Leo moon, one that calls for us to sit in the burning core of our histories and be tempered into something new, to become stronger by allowing the false parts of ourselves to be burned away. It calls for us to keep changing and moving forward by looking at what has always seemed too painful to face, to stop believing in the weaker versions of ourselves and step into the skin of our deeper strengths.

I'm no longer in a back brace as I sit here and type. I no longer have to, but will always fall to my knees and give gratitude for all I've been given, especially in the wake of facing the pain of my family, and the pain of all I've ever tried to deny about myself. I fall to my knees for love, for the now, for the future. My gratitude and love flow freely, unobstructed now. And mixed with this love is sorrow. I can feel now how these things are part of one another, and in feeling them all at once, I can more clearly see myself.

There are so many ways in which I was raised to *not* see all the injustice going on around me, to accept all the benefits and privileges of being born in America in 1988 as a white "male" individual, as if I had earned them all on my own. But I was born on ground that depends on the oppression and domination of most of the people on this planet. I spent most of my life not knowing this.

Coming to realize we've been unable to see and feel things that are apparent to others is painful, but this is part of what I mean by "sitting in the burning core of our histories." This is what I mean by becoming stronger than we think we are—the strength to set aside our egos so that we can change ourselves and change the world. The strength to relate to people, to *see* and *feel*, to step into our lives and reclaim the humanity that we have been forced to exchange for material and cultural privilege, *without* our consent.

Through the process of writing, I've come to new realizations about myself—and this process will continue. I might later look back on things I've said and see clearly how my privilege has obscured my vision. That's okay. What matters isn't that we get things wrong, or that we don't see every angle—that's just part of being a person. What matters is how we *respond* to it, and allow ourselves to be changed by it. How humble we can be to accept our mistakes and move forward, embracing that new knowledge with gratitude. It's all part of learning how to be human in a system that has made all of us less than human, no matter where we're standing.

Right now, it's 2019, and a reality-star real-estate mogul is president of the United States of America. While some folks are still asking *how* this could have happened, it makes perfect sense to me. It's the logical conclusion when a moral order places capital—not truth or justice or people—at its center. The Trump administration has made overt again the white supremacy on which this country was founded, and if you scratch the surface of history just a little, it's easy to see how what we understand as "race" was invented as a moral justification for the economic model of slavery, the genocide of indigenous people, and the theft of an entire continent. This is the history that has made the present. We're all born into a vast interconnected network of material and spiritual traumas. These are different for each of us, depending on how and where we were born, and I think it's necessary to see how these differences are part of the same historical process that has led us to where we are now: a country of massive economic disparity, environmental devastation, mass incarceration, and the state-sanctioned murder and oppression of Black people and other people of color, immigrants, queer and trans people, women, and *all* poor people.

The optimist in me refuses to believe that we can't overcome our past and change the future. The world is as beautiful as it is worrisome these days. But we still have miracles and lessons and freedoms and the ability to help those in need. We have hope and grace, and we have love. We have one another, and we have ourselves, as long as we love ourselves. We have the ability to heal, to transform, to effect change—to *be* change and be changed.

Through my processes of embracing my queerness and gender identity, of getting sober from alcohol and healing the wounds that came from both family and society, I've come to realize more and more how important finding one's spirituality is. This society has attempted to take even this away from us, to commodify our relationship to that which is larger than us and sell it back to us. But communing with the spirits is a way to tap into history, to feel how both ourselves and the times we live in now are products of everything that has come before us. The spirits know that something is deeply wrong here, that the world we are living in currently is the wrong one. For white people, in particular, it's especially important to come to understand this, to change ourselves so that we can effectively work with others to move the tide of history in a different direction—away from a story in which white people are at the center, where capital matters more than the planet. The Ghost Dance—the collective spiritual movement and last stand of American Indians before the United States government wiped out organized indigenous resistance in the 1880s—prophesied the devastation we are now seeing come to pass. In order to make our own prophecies, to envision and work toward a different future, we have to listen to our spirits, and use what we see and hear to come together to fight for a new world, for all of us.

For now, I'm doing what I can in this fight as a purveyor of pop culture. If my life journey had gone differently—say, if I'd chosen to be a painter—a lot fewer people would be listening to me now. I wanted to be famous for so long, and I wanted to make money. And then my life got all fucked up when I allowed money to stand in place of my heart. My moral center moved far away from me, and I hurt myself and everyone around me. It was only when I placed truth and humanity, rather than fame and capital, back at the core of my beliefs and actions that I was able to essentially heal.

My newfound spiritual and political consciousness has demanded that I rethink this idea of fame and what it means to me. Over the years, my addiction to celebrity unlocked all these other parts of myself that manifested as pain and dependency. The more famous people get, the more they lose sight of what really matters. Hollywood is an industry run on capital—not truth, justice, or even people. Which is precisely why only a select few make it, and even fewer have real longevity. In the modern world of social media, our entire life experience is commodified by likes and comments. But my happiness, my wholeness, no longer depends on accolades and recognition to validate my experience. My life is constantly shifting, and now that I have more of a sense of what really matters, I am able to see more clearly. I am in a perpetual state of fluid motion, astral traveling to every corner of the universe, and enjoying the ride through the vast space between.

I don't know exactly what's in store for the future. I don't know what my future relationships—platonic, romantic, familial, or spiritual—are going to look like, but I know that I will continue to be inspired by human beings. I know that I will continue to be inspired by this planet, the elements, the natural world, and the endless animal and plant spirits and teachers who reveal themselves to me. I know that I have great teachers and lovers in the friends I hold, the people who hold me, and the ones who have yet to come into my life. I know that I have my best friend in the universe, no matter what, in this lifetime and the ones to follow. Bethany, *baby, baby, baby*, I love you. I don't have all the answers on how Bethany and I are going to manage our polyamorous marriage, privately or publicly, especially when we throw kids into the mix. Being a parent is the one absolute, and I want them to know that I did everything, all of it, for love. All of it, for you.

I know that my family will always be my family, and some days will be better than others. But no matter what, I love all of them. My uncle specifically has been such a foundational figure in my life. He taught me how to heal through alternative spiritual practices, and in some ways, I am continuing his legacy. I've learned that infinite transformation is possible—people are capable of change, and that change comes from the least likely of places. I never thought I would be the person I am now, and that fuels so much of the work I do.

I know wholeheartedly that there is more good than evil in

the world. I know that in the fields of social justice and activism, we must show up for ourselves first, and only then will we be able to show up for others. And I know that I'm going to continue to share my creative expressions. Art has the power to change us, to change the world, as we begin to imagine what isn't possible yet. We all run to things that feel temporary and that are numbing, but we have to feel the pain in order to truly heal. We have to hit the bottom before we even are able to recognize the top. My addictions surfaced because of deep-rooted abandonment issues, my own gender and sexuality, my struggle with celebrity. At the end of the day, it took me actually getting fucked up to deal with my queerness.

We are all storytellers in some capacity; that is how we survive. Telling stories is what reminds us to live. And as storytellers, we should make our stories passionate and impactful, make them vulnerable, make them colorful, make them count, make them about love, with love, for love. My hope is that by telling my story, I have helped foster love and understanding for diverse perspectives by honoring the space between that connects all of us. It is in this space that true healing happens. And just as I try to find the last sentence of a story without an ending, I remember the work is always never ending. I am never ending. You are never ending. There is still so much more work to be done.

The space between everything, all of it is you.

All *love*, it is you.

Nico Tortorella is an actor, television personality, and author of the poetry collection *all of it is you*. Nico stars in the hit series *Younger* and is an outspoken advocate for the LGBTQIA+ community. They live in New York.

## ABOUT THE TYPE

This book was set in Legacy, a typeface family designed by Ronald Arnholm (b. 1939) and issued in digital form by ITC in 1992. Both its serifed and unserifed versions are based on an original type created by the French punchcutter Nicholas Jenson in the late fifteenth century. While Legacy tends to differ from Jenson's original in its proportions, it maintains much of the latter's characteristic modulations in stroke.